Elmgreen & Dragset
BIOGRAPHY

ELMGREEN & DRAGSET

Essays and interviews by Andrew Berardini • Iwona Blazwick • Susanne Christensen • Ruth Direktor • Bruce Willis Ferguson • Massimiliano Gioni • Martin Herbert • Shannon Jackson • Gunnar B. Kvaran • Quinn Latimer • Hans Ulrich Obrist • Marianne Torp

ARCHIVE BOOKS

TABLE OF CONTENTS

Foreword

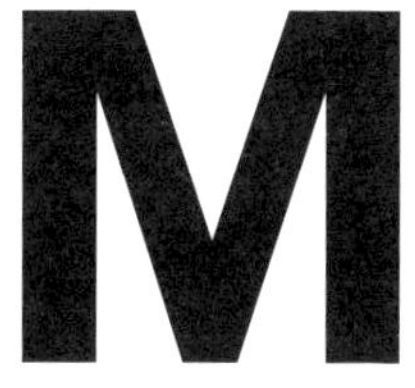

Much has been written about Elmgreen & Dragset's art in the nearly twenty years that have passed since they first started working together on the international art scene. Eminent curators, scholars and theoreticians have contributed to the understanding of a body of work that has transformed the function and perception of spaces, structures and architecture in numerous ways, emphasising that our public space is not a neutral zone, but rather a battleground of diverging desires.

In conjunction with the three-part exhibition series 'Biography' presented at Astrup Fearnley Museet in Oslo, the SMK National Gallery of Denmark in Copenhagen and at the Tel Aviv Museum of Art in Tel Aviv, we have brought together some of today's leading writers to cast light on different aspects of Elmgreen & Dragset's artistic practice. With their most recent exhibition, the artists have posed questions related to the constitution of an identity. What are the conditions that define the 'self' when we can no longer clearly map and differentiate our individual identities through binary oppositions and 'otherness'? Biographical and fictitious identities connect seamlessly within the various strands of narratives defining the artists' work. In 'Biography', it is the personal, the exceptional and the disaffected that are used in the artists' subjective examination of what we consider common or universal.

Elmgreen & Dragset investigate this notion of the biographical by placing existing works in different constellations and thus introducing a multitude of layers to the already existing narratives. We have invited a number of writers to further expand our thoughts on this remarkable artistic practice. The reader includes new texts by Andrew Berardini, Iwona Blazwick, Susanne Christensen, Ruth Direktor, Bruce Willis Ferguson, Quinn Latimer and Marianne Torp. The artists discuss their past and current work in a new interview with Hans Ulrich Obrist and an already published interview by myself done in conjunction with the exhibition 'Biography' in Oslo. Previously published texts by Massimiliano Gioni, Martin Herbert and Shannon Jackson, as well as a 1998 interview by Obrist, have been included upon the wish of the artists and the editors. These might function in the same way as the artworks in the exhibition: by experiencing existing works in new contexts, we might gain new insights.

Gunnar B. Kvaran
Director, Astrup Fearnley Museet

Hyper Repetitions
Elmgreen & Dragset's
Exhibition-Installations

MARIANNE TORP

'If you're trapped in the dream of the other, you're fucked.'[1]

Over the last ten years, Elmgreen & Dragset have created large, carefully choreographed exhibition projects such as 'The Welfare Show' (2005–6), 'Home is the Place You Left' (2008), 'The Collectors' (2009), 'Celebrity – The One & The Many' (2010–11) and 'Tomorrow' (2013) that bring together various permutations of existing works from their oeuvre in a kind of 'total installation'.[2] In 2014–15, the Astrup Fearnley Museet in Oslo, the SMK National Gallery of Denmark in Copenhagen, and the Tel Aviv Museum of Art in Tel Aviv are each showing an instalment of the exhibition trilogy 'Biography', also based on an installation-like presentation of existing and new works.

These large-scale exhibition-installations shift the focus away from individual works and onto the totality that they constitute together or, as Michael Elmgreen puts it in an interview with Gunnar B. Kvaran: 'every time we do an exhibition, we don't consider it just a collection of artworks, but as an artwork in itself: the exhibition is the work'.[3] The exhibitions take place within architectural structures that are either built as autonomous rooms in the venue's galleries, or which modify and appropriate the existing architecture. Within these structures, Elmgreen & Dragset place their own and sometimes other artists' works, often sculptural objects that take the form of hyperrealistic wax figures, modified pieces of furniture, architectural structures and constructed functional objects. The nature of the works often renders all other staging and set-dressing obsolete. This is emphatically *not* exhibition architecture in the traditional vein, creating a 'neutral' setting to support the works on display; rather, these structures are works of art in themselves, merging to form a conceptual and spatial unity. In that sense, the exhibitions invite observers to enter a complex universe that seems to refer to some underlying narrative and is simultaneously an installation of artworks *and* an art installation. The individual sculptures serve a double function as works in the exhibition and as objects that are combined with other objects to create the overall situation that constitutes the final installation. The artists themselves have often compared their exhibitions to a film set that helps stage a story, and from this perspective the spectator becomes a protagonist who acts in the film without full knowledge of the script.

I use the term 'exhibition-installations' in order to acknowledge the distinctive position of these projects, poised between exhibition and installation. However, they share a number of traits with what, referring to his own practice from the 1990s, Ilya Kabakov defined as 'total installations', in which he used existing materials and objects to create detailed installations with a strong narrative point of departure. In her book *Installation Art*, the British art historian and critic Claire Bishop has defined various types of installations, calling those in the vein of Kabakov's total installations 'the dream scene'. This term is based on Freud's definition of the three main features of dreams: 'the sensory immediacy of conscious perception, a composite structure, and the elucidation of meaning through free-association'.[4] It seems helpful in relation to Elmgreen & Dragset's exhibition-installations, where, as in a dream, you find yourself in a situation that you *experience*, rather than consciously intellectualise, through your own subjective associations, references and fantasies triggered by the assemblage of visual signs, cues, and objects that you encounter along the way. Like a dream, this composite structure cannot be decoded by rational means; it can only be grasped in an associative manner through each individual's 'affective and verbal connections'.[5] Even though these exhibition-installations are far removed from Kabakov's total installations in terms of their overall mood and expression, they nevertheless share these dreamlike qualities and a strong narrative element that clearly structures the installation, but which nevertheless remains partially hidden and ambiguous.

However, while Kabakov incorporates existing objects and materials into his installations, Elmgreen & Dragset's installations are also – and sometimes exclusively – based on the re-contextualisation of existing *artworks*.

In this text, I will explore the devices and approaches used in these scenarios. In particular, I will look at how they establish themselves as immediately recognisable segments of 'reality', and will consider the implications of this in relation to our experience of the installations, discussing how they create a framework that allows for reusing – or repeating – existing works, and the potential in this approach for critical change. The French philosophers Gilles Deleuze and Félix Guattari have often been cited as a reference for the discussion of Elmgreen & Dragset's works, especially their theories of deterritorialisation and the nomadic.[6] Here, I will focus on Deleuze's theories of repetition and difference, which are useful for the discussion of the recurrent use of existing works in Elmgreen & Dragset's praxis. I will also touch upon other philosophical positions that seem particularly relevant to the socio-critical perspective characteristic of the artists' work, such as the theories of the real coined by postmodern theorists like the French philosopher Jean Baudrillard and his Italian colleague Mario Perniola.

The complexities of recognisability

As observers, we willingly – even eagerly – allow ourselves to be lured into Emgreen & Dragset's exhibitions. Ballrooms and dining rooms, bedrooms, bars and high-rise buildings form hyper-detailed spaces and environments into which we can let ourselves be seduced.[7]

This immediate seduction is later replaced by a conscious reflection, which I will discuss later. Here, I wish to focus on how the artists employ the effect of immediate recognisability in relation to the observer. You seem to step directly from the galleries of a museum into a private home, for example, in the exhibition 'Tomorrow' (2013) **[ill. 1–8]**, or to move from a commercial gallery into an abandoned gay bar in *The Mirror* (2008) **[ill. 20–22]**, and a calming sense of familiarity initially blurs the transition from 'reality' to art installation. Or you may be unwittingly placed in the position of an intruder when you suddenly find yourself in the middle of a private flat where the absent host's letters are left out in full view on his desk, and his personal belongings are displayed in the bedroom. Similarly, your curiosity is piqued beyond resistance by the lit windows in a tenement building in 'The One & The Many' (2010) **[ill. 9]**, or by the acts taking place behind photo-booth curtains or public-toilet doors in *Photo Booth* (2001) and *Occupied/Powerless Structures, Fig. 143* (2001).

This is to say that the immediate, seductive appeal of the large exhibition-installations derives from their reassuring recognisability. However, it soon turns out that the scenarios do not fully replicate or repeat the 'reality' they resemble, and the tableaus and environments are not as immediately conceptually accessible as you were at first led to believe. It is difficult to fully decode the situations – are the rooms and the homes real or staged? Are the rooms private or public? Are you an invited guest or an unwanted trespasser?

There is, in other words, something suspect underlying the premise. In this sense, the exhibitions convey a fundamental complexity: Elmgreen & Dragset deliberately undermine the immediate promise of a rapid and unambiguous resolution and point to the more complicated levels of meaning that essentially infuse all human experience.

The narratives in Elmgreen & Dragset's works and installations, and in their exhibitions as a whole, all support this experience of ambivalence. They are carefully orchestrated, mimicking the reality of which they seem to be a segment in such detail that they prompt us to expect a narrative resolution that we can fully decipher and understand. However, the various clues and tracks – laid down with such care and deliberation – turn out to branch wildly or end up in dead ends. We can never be entirely sure who inhabits the rooms through which we move, nor of what has taken place prior to the fateful or fatal situations we come across as we pass through the exhibition-installation. Massimiliano Gioni has described this shift in the experience of Elmgreen & Dragset's work as a situation of desire: 'In their work you are often left yearning for something that is constantly out of reach or kept at a distance: theirs is not an aesthetics of relations – it is an aesthetics of longing and desire.'[8] Through this destabilisation of recognisability and decipherability, Elmgreen & Dragset point to an underlying complexity as a fundamental condition of contemporary existence in which values change rapidly, social categories dissolve and formerly separated lifestyles interchange.

Simulacra

Elmgreen & Dragset's installations never seek to veil their artificiality or their nature as constructs. They deliberately undermine the illusionism to which at first glance they seem to aspire through certain elements that have been modified, stylised or processed, or strangely placed objects that disrupt their unity. As the artists put it: 'The fact that our installations are not "real-real" is quite deliberate; rather, they represent an idea of, for example, a home. In this regard we're inspired by Hammershøi's paintings of interiors; they too aren't realistic, but act as renditions of mental states.'[9]

Elmgreen & Dragset's two pavilions at the Venice Biennale **[ill. 14–19]** positioned themselves in this borderland, where closer inspection of the seemingly realistic interiors revealed symbolic and dysfunctional features, such as a dining table that has been split in two **[ill. 19]** or a crumbling staircase, or staged performers such as a naked man calmly reading a book while lounging, entirely unperturbed, on a piece of luxury furniture **[ill. 16]**. Precisely because these installations do not simply repeat or copy reality, they transcend representation and come to exist in their own right instead, constituting a reality of their own. As Baudrillard claims, when we can no longer distinguish between reality and non-reality, the two are replaced by 'hyperreality': 'The hyperreal represents a much more advanced phase, in the sense that even the contradiction between the real and the imaginary is effaced. The unreal is no longer that of a dream or of a fantasy, of a beyond or a within, it is that of *hallucinatory resemblance of the real with itself.*'[10]

Baudrillard wrote his famous essays on simulacra in 1981, an age when the information flow generated by mass media was growing exponentially. In many respects his theory has taken on additional relevance today, now that the distribution and mediation of information via the internet has added an extra dimension to the representation of the real. Similarly, the pervasive culture of self-staging represented by reality TV and internet-based social networks has served to blur the boundaries between reality and representation even further, all the way down to the level of the construction of one's own identity. Each individual's opportunity to create an edited and staged self-image on such platforms – a 'virtual simulacrum' – is a strong thematic aspect of many of Elmgreen & Dragset's works. This is very evident in the habits of the fictitious inhabitants of the council house featured in the installation 'The One & The Many', who are watching *Idol* on TV, have a karaoke machine running, and are creating a dating profile (which happens to be authentic, by the way) [ill. **9–10**]. To put it briefly, the artists are interested in what Elmgreen has called 'an instant reality',[11] which replaces physical, relational communities.

Baudrillard regarded simulation as a symptom of a negative social and cultural development where 'the real' has become so mediated that the mediated version seems more real than reality itself. When signs no longer refer to an outside reality but exist in their own right, they become simulacra. Deleuze defines the simulacrum more positively, perceiving it as an ongoing series of repeated repetitions:

'However, in the infinite movement of degraded likeness from copy to copy, we reach a point at which everything changes nature, at which copies themselves flip over into simulacra and at which, finally, resemblance or spiritual imitation gives way to repetition.'[12] In his theory of difference and repetition, the simulacrum has the potential to effect a break with norms and conventions. The very possibility of change resides in the recognition of difference.

Repetition

In Elmgreen & Dragset's exhibition-installations, individual sculptures are re-contextualised in changing exhibitions. Among the works that they have re-used – or repeated – are *Queer Bar/Powerless Structures, Fig. 21* (1998); *Marriage* (2004); *Modern Moses* (2006) [ill. 45]; *It's The Small Things in Life That Really Matter, Blah, Blah, Blah* (2006) [ill. 46]; *Andrea Candela* (2006) [ill. 23]; *The Mirror* (2008) [ill. 20–22]; *Table for Bergman* (2009) [ill. 19]; *Death of a Collector* (2009) [ill. 15]; *Untitled (The Mysterious Afterlife of Mr B)* (2011) [ill. 24] and *The Future* (2013), to mention just a few. The inherent ambiguity of these individual works is what makes it possible to situate them in different contexts. Such recycling and recirculation increases their complexity as you find yourself experiencing them in different contexts. In other words, each exhibition situates the repeated works in such a manner that they establish a difference. As Deleuze has noted, an inherent feature of repetition is a paradoxical emancipation from norm and convention, since repetition unavoidably establishes a difference from what it repeats, thereby distancing itself from the original: 'Systems in which different relates to different through difference itself are systems of simulacra.

Such systems are intensive; they rest ultimately upon the
nature of intensive quantities, which precisely communicate
through their differences.'[13]

Deleuze, then, sees difference as the point where something else becomes possible by virtue of the shifts and
varying conditions involved in any repetition. One might
argue that Elmgreen & Dragset's practice of repeatedly
reusing the same sculpture in different exhibitions points
to the differences that arise between various readings
of the works. As Deleuze claims, repetition creates the
basis for new knowledge, new insight. By letting the
same work repeatedly enter into new contexts the artists
allow individual works to take on new meaning, or
certainly different shades of meaning. In doing so, they
not only break down the autonomy of individual works,
but also the unambiguous reading of the work. When
the dead man floating in a pool in *Death of a Collector*
(2009) is moved from the travertine terrace of a fancy
residence to a gloomy roadside motel environment,
the narrative implications change radically. Likewise,
when the gilded maid *Rosa* (2006) is transported from
what appears to be a private family house in the Danish
Pavilion **[ill. 18]** to a museum gallery in the form of her
counterpart *Irina* (2007) standing in front of a series of
monochromes in the Astrup Fearnley Museet **[ill. 32]**,
the relocation changes the reading of the maid. From
being a silent, obedient servant with her hands folded
at her back, she becomes an attentive and contemplative
museum visitor, re-enacting the normative position
of an appreciative and privileged cultural consumer.

Through these kinds of repetitions of their works, Elmgreen & Dragset not only establish a subtle social critique, but, on a more abstract level, they also point to the potential of the artwork in terms of complex meaning, and to how the context informs any reading.

Perniola has also touched upon the relation between repetition and simulacrum. Rather than representing a loss of reality, he regards the simulacrum as a potential extension of the basis for experience and knowledge, and tries to update the definition of art as an operation rather than a production or cognition. He argues that this operational understanding must be closely linked to the concept of simulacrum, claiming that art succeeds in becoming operational when it is 'a simulatory, mimetic operation executed with the intention of imitating a reality, an original, or a model with such completeness that its originality and privileged position – in a word its essence – is dissolved.'[14] Such an operation takes place in Elmgreen & Dragset's installation-exhibitions. They become simulacras through their painstakingly repetition of reality, and precisely because they are so successful in this venture manage to reach beyond the reality they appear to mimic. This transgression manifests itself in the ambivalence with which you as viewer strive to grasp the situation and often end up finding the alluring reality of the scenes and tableaus weirdly unfamiliar. According to Perniola's argument, this occurs because the original models are suspended, taken out of the equation. Instead, a simulacrum constitutes itself, replacing the reality it originally imitated.

Thus Elmgreen & Dragset's exhibition-installations succeed in carrying out what Baudrillard describes as 'a question of substituting signs of the real for the real itself'.[15]

In a sense, the recurring use of existing sculptures in ever-new installation contexts is a way of challenging their uniqueness, thereby also questioning the autonomy that we often attribute to the individual work. This depletion is closely connected to the conceptual basis of the ongoing *Powerless Structures* series, begun in 1997.

Powerless Structures

The works in the *Powerless Structures* series are linked by their shared title, but are individually numbered as 'figures', meaning that they become a materialisation or visualisation of an overall abstract structure, a kind of model. The numbering of these 'figures' is not consecutive but completely random, so that even the structure that might have resided in a chronological numbering is made powerless.

The large exhibition-installations seem to be linked to conceptual aspects of *Powerless Structures* and may perhaps be read as a reflection of the strategies at play in the series. The works in *Powerless Structures* often take their point of departure from the power structures associated with institutions such as the prison, as in *Prison Breaking/Powerless Structures. Fig 333* (2002) **[ill. 38]**; the gallery, as in *Elevated Gallery/ Powerless Structures, Fig. 146* (2001) **[ill. 39]**; or the museum, as in *Powerless Structures, Fig. 529* (2014) **[ill. 31]**. Inspired by French philosopher Michel Foucault, Elmgreen & Dragset have sought to render visible the behavioural adjustment –

or disciplining, as Foucault would call it – embedded in such institutions and in the social, economic and hierarchical technologies associated with them. They are interested in how accepted and well-established structures can be destabilised through repetition based on re-presentations of recognisable forms, thereby offering a critique of those same forms (familiar institutional architecture or well-established sculptural categories, for example). In a sense, this gesture encompasses the artists' entire body of work. One might argue that by repeating the same works in different exhibition-installations they deliberately destabilise the very power structure that characterises a well established and acclaimed body of artistic work.

Elmgreen & Dragset's exhibition-installations may, then, be viewed in light of their intentions with *Powerless Structures*. The critical potential pertaining to the destabilisation of familiar structures and thus the implied possibility of reinvention and change, is a central feature of the series. The exhibition-installations do the same thing: they dissolve the relationship between the work and the institution's architecture, between spectator and artwork, and between the artwork and the oeuvre. According to Bishop, a fundamental destabilisation of the conventional relation between the viewer (or the subject) and the artwork is a key feature of installation art. Rather than a relation based on the beholder's physical separation from the work, installation art provides a fundamentally different experience: 'traditional single-point perspective is overturned by installation art's plural and fragmented vistas: as a result, our hierarchical and centred relation to the work of art (and to ourselves) is undermined and destabilised.'[16]

Such destabilisation is not only characteristic of the viewing experience itself, but also encompasses our relationship with ourselves and hence how we experience Elmgreen & Dragset's exhibition-installations, which act as catalysts for a kind of simultaneous affirmation *and* depletion of the meaning of the autonomous work. At the same time, the works seem to destabilise the exhibition setting – the institution – from the inside, like a virus. They thus establish an ambiguous, double move that at the same time affirms and dissolves the very structures of institution, exhibition and artwork.

Elmgreen & Dragset neither repeat nor represent the real; rather, they create new realities in the form of hyperreal environments and tableaus that open up opportunities for critical reflection. 'Biography' consists of three individual exhibitions that continue the artists' exploration of the exhibition-installation structure and share a certain number of works that will reappear in different combinations in the trillogy. In these shows Elmgreen & Dragset are continuing their exploration of the potential of hyperreality and repetition, and of how these two features mutually support each other. By repeating reality, they blur the differences between the 'original real' and their continuously repeated versions. Likewise, the repetition of their own artworks establishes an awareness of the implications of the differences in terms of connotations and meanings that become evident through the very act of repetition. These differences come to establish a ground for a more general, critical reflection upon the act of experiencing.

This text has been peer-reviewed.

[1] This oft-quoted truism is attributed to Gilles Deleuze.

[2] Elmgreen & Dragset have created the following exhibition-installations: 'The Welfare Show', four different versions of which were shown at Bergen Kunsthall, 2005, BAWAG Foundation, Vienna, 2005, Serpentine Gallery, London, 2006 and The Power Plant, Toronto, 2006; 'Home is the Place You Left', Trondheim Kunstmuseum, 2008; 'The Collectors', The Danish and Nordic Pavilions, 53rd Venice Biennale, 2009. In 2010–11 Elmgreen & Dragset staged two versions of an exhibition, each bearing its own title variant, 'Celebrity – The One & The Many', ZKM, Karlsruhe, and 'The One & The Many', Museum Boijmans Van Beuningen and the Port of Rotterdam/ former Submarine Wharf in Rotterdam's harbour. The exhibition 'Tomorrow' was shown at the V&A in London, 2013.

[3] Michael Elmgreen in an interview with Ingar Dragset and Gunnar B. Kvaran, 'Whose Biography?' in *Elmgreen & Dragset – Biography*, exhibition catalogue, Astrup Fearnley Museet, 2014, p.39, reprinted in this publication, pp.35-51.

[4] Claire Bishop, *Installation Art. A Critical History*, Tate Publishing, London, 2005, p.16.

[5] Ibid.

[6] See for instance, Sanne Kofod Olsen, 'Transgressive Spaces', in *Powerless Structures – works by Michael Elmgreen and Ingar Dragset*, Nifca, Helsinki, 1998, pp.4-23; Marianne Torp, *Michael Elmgreen and Ingar Dragset. A Room Defined by its Accessibility*, x-rummet, SMK, 2001.

[7] Martin Hartung has examined the voyeuristic aspect of this position of the spectator within the total installations of Elmgreen & Dragset in Peter Weibel and Andreas F. Beitin (ed.), 'Staging the Spectator', *Elmgreen & Dragset: Triology*, Verlag der Buchhandlung Walther König, Cologne, 2011, pp.88-101.

8 Massimiliano Gioni, 'The Erotic Frigidaire', in *Elmgreen & Dragset: This is the First Day of My Life*, Hatje Cantz Verlag, Ostfildern, 2008, p.10, reprinted in this publication, pp.153-9.

9 Michael Elmgreen and Ingar Dragset in conversation, 29 April 2014.

10 Jean Baudrillard, 'The Order of Simulacra', in *Simulations*, Semiotext(e), 1983, p.142, first published in *Simulacre et Simulations*, 1981.

11 Michael Elmgreen and Ingar Dragset in conversation with the author, 29 April 2014.

12 Gilles Deleuze, *Difference and Repetition* (1968), Columbia University Press, New York, 1994, p.128.

13 Ibid., p.277.

14 Mario Perniola, 'Kunsten som mimetisk operation', *Blændværker*, Sjakalen, 1982, p.62 (author's translation); http://plato.stanford.edu/entries/postmodernism/#4.

15 Baudrillard, 'The Precession of Simulacra', in op. cit., p.4.

16 Bishop, op. cit., p.47.

Biographical, Too Biographical

RUTH DIREKTOR

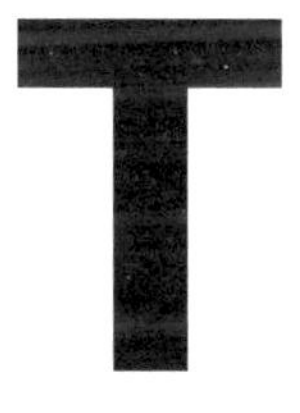he first art-history book of the New Era was published in 1550 under the title *The Lives of the Most Eminent Painters, Sculptors and Architects*. Over the years, for the sake of convenience, Giorgio Vasari's book came to be known as the *Lives*. It featured some 200 artists from Early to High Renaissance, the description of whose work was not merely intertwined with the stories of their lives, but guided by and presented through them. The tradition on which Vasari drew was based on the fantastic chronicles of the gods in Greek and Roman mythology, which were transformed into the stories of the Christian saints, and ultimately incarnated in the life stories of the luminaries of Renaissance humanism. Viewed through the prism of modern consciousness, these stories often seem like unfounded rumours or legends, passed on by word of mouth. Thus largely unauthenticated and mythologised biographies verging on the invented are the foundation on which the written history of art in modern times was based.

Simplistic? Gossipy? Outdated? No wonder art scholars tend to regard the *Lives* with some measure of suspicion. And no wonder that almost 500 years after Vasari's *Lives*, when Elmgreen & Dragset choose to entitle their grand project 'Biography', their use of the word, with its implied content, can only be seen as defiant or ironic. With 'Biography', Elmgreen & Dragset bring their (real, fictive, invented, presumed or imaginary) biography to centre stage. And by highlighting certain institutional elements of the large, amorphous entity called the art world – 'Museum', 'White Cube', 'Collector', 'Critic' – they lead the viewer to the backstage of artistic creation. But through the simple fact that their works are signed by two names, they subvert the very term 'Biography'.

This takes us back to Vasari, the author largely responsible for constituting the aura around the One – the genius, individual artist. The artists about whom he writes might have worked in large studios with many assistants, but this arrangement was based on a clear hierarchy: the master and his apprentices. Vasari's division of his book into chapters by artist not only assumes the cataloguing and sorting underlying modern art history, but also the artist as the most significant perspective. The divisions could have been different – for example, by city, medium, subject matter – but as a Renaissance humanist, Vasari centres his writing on the human element – and on the One. The one who is the extraordinary artist. The young Giotto working for Cimabue drew a fly on a painting by his master that was so lifelike that the latter tried to chase it away; Leonardo had such an urbane, graceful and sociable personality that he was admired by everyone and so on …

And alongside being gifted individuals, the protagonists of the *Lives* possess other self-evident characteristics: they are white males of the lower or middle classes. Those who did not meet these requirements – women, for example, or non-European men – had no one to write their chronicles.

Two-who-work-together undermines the myth of the individual. Thus the emergence of artist duos who exhibit under a shared signature towards the end of the twentieth century subverts one of the most deeply rooted perceptions of the art world. The two emerge as a unit; as some*thing*, rather than some*one*. The most quintessential artist duo of contemporary art – Gilbert & George – further undermined expectations as a gay couple who externalised their dual portrait throughout their body of work. They began their career in 1969, performing a song by the British comedy duo Flanagan and Allen, 'Underneath the Arches', about two homeless nomads who find solace in life's small pleasures. Put in Gilbert & George's mouths, with their metallic-coloured faces and robotic gestures, the song acquired the shift into oddity that would inform their entire oeuvre, the work of two-instead-of-one.

Before Gilbert & George came another famous artist duo, Bernd and Hilla Becher, who began working together in 1959. Their heterosexual relationship, and the fact that each had worked individually for a short period before they met, as well as the highly non-subjective nature of their joint work, represents a near-antithetical version of Gilbert & George's coupled artistic oeuvre: an anonymous, sterile, impersonal photographic life project.

The Bechers' photography strove to be as objective as possible, while effacing the identities of those behind the camera. Their joint signature, however, like that of any artist duo, is inevitably pushed into the centre of our visual field. In the case of the Bechers, it guides the gaze observing their monumental body of photographs to the oscillation between the one and the many (to borrow an exhibition title from Elmgreen & Dragset): the movement between the singular image and multiple images; between the archetype and its variations.

The Bechers and Gilbert & George represent two archetypes of the artist duo. In the work of the former, the biographical element is implicit (yet bursts forth through the works if one so much as reflects on it), while in the work of the latter, it is explicit (although, of course, only as explicit as the artists choose to make it). In Elmgreen & Dragset's work, the biographical element is at once explicit and implicit, and it is almost always tied, in various ways, to their relationship and their dual identity as artists. Thus, for instance, in their short play, *Happy Days in the Art World* **[ill. 52]** (staged as part of Performa 11, 2011), the protagonists are two artists working together, concerned about what will happen to their creative future if they break up. Elmgreen & Dragset did indeed break up as a romantic couple, yet have continued working together as artists, thus adding an unprecedented line to their biography. Their exhibition 'Celebrity – The One & The Many' **[ill. 9–13]** (at ZKM, Karlsruhe, 2010–11) centred on the link between the general population and celebrities chased by the paparazzi who write their photographic biographies.

Thus the immediate reading of 'The One & The Many' is the celebrated one versus the many observing him. In the context of the duo, however, the one must be regarded as made up of inseparable parts. The one is never just one, monolithic, unique, singular, consistent and coherent. The one is the many. The one may be the Collectors (the protagonists of Elmgreen & Dragset's work by that name at the 53rd Venice Biennale, 2009) **[ill. 14–19]**; or it may emerge elusively under the name of Sturtevant – in herself, one who is many – whose presence at the Danish Pavilion further jolted the persona of artists/collectors/curators assumed by Elmgreen & Dragset: a painting by Frank Stella or Sturtevant masquerading as Stella? A work by Maurizio Cattelan or perhaps another masquerade? Who are the artists behind these works?

Elmgreen & Dragset's presentation in two neighbouring national pavilions at the Giardini – the Danish and the Nordic – in itself emphasised the aspect of the one who is at least two, if not more. The self-portrait, like the solo show, like the unique biography (the monograph), is deconstructed, dissolving into a dual, stratified and multiple self-portrait. In this respect, the dead body floating face down in a swimming pool outside the Nordic Pavilion, entitled *Death of a Collector* **[ill. 15]**, echoes the cliché of the 'Death of the Author'. The man in black trousers and a white shirt, whose shoes are sitting on the edge of the pool, is a modern everyman, although a privileged one (his shoes are Prada; his residence is full of artifacts and stylish designer pieces). The beautiful modernist structure behind him functions as the perfect backdrop for the photogenic death of Mr B, Mr Biography, Mr One.

Elmgreen & Dragset's modus operandi is obviously not without twists. Rather than eliminating the biographical from art, they introduce an enhanced version of the traditional artistic life story as coined by Vasari and later abandoned by his successors. They seem to go back to it only to extract its trickling between the canonical and the anecdotal, the pivotal and non-essential. Their emphasis on the biographical aspect underscores the life story as a marginal discourse whose significance is inferior to writing based on facts or ideas, and it is through the use of this binary opposition at the core of modern thought that an additional identification is implied – the biographical discourse is a kind of gossip, and hence it is linked to the feminine.

Vasari's lost honour can be retrieved within postmodern thought, which upturns every stone in the modernist foundation of the right and the worthy. To relativist, doubting eyes, the narrated biography might be perceived as potentially confrontational. And indeed, in accordance with this way of thinking, back in 1996, visual culture scholar Irit Rogoff wrote in favour of gossip.[1] By proposing that we regard speech that is not necessarily authorised as a possible source of truth, and by relying on gossip as a form of 'postmodern testimony', she set out to dissolve the hierarchy between truth and falsehood, and in fact between the credible and the incredible. Rogoff discussed gossip in the feminist context as a mode of relational knowledge that can oppose the prevalent, hegemonic discourse. Approximately a decade later, art writer Gavin Butt took Rogoff's insights one step further, placing gossip in the homosexual context by examining the web of gossip and rumours about gay artists in 1950s and 1960s New York, when sexual identity was still not discussed out loud.[2] He tied gossip to rumours of homosexuality by virtue of the fact that it is information perceived as scandalous, hence bound to be handed down by word of mouth, to be whispered, rather than published. The rumours about a biographical detail – whether to do with sexual identity or not – infiltrate the official narrative of the artist.

One may also refer here to Israeli historian Dr Yuval Noah Harari in *Sapiens: A Brief History of Humankind*, where he identified gossip as a key factor in transforming Homo sapiens around 70,000 years ago into what it is today: the most dominant creature on Earth.[3] Despite the physical inferiority of our ancestors, Harari maintained, they were advantaged by their linguistic superiority, discernible in the ability – and desire – to discuss things that were not entirely purposeful, task-oriented, or vital for immediate survival. Survivalist speech, for instance, would be 'Lion on the right', 'Storm approaching', 'Fire in the forest'. Homo sapiens, however, wished to convey a different type of information too – to tell someone about a third party, to relate what he saw, or what he heard. According to Harari, these stories – namely gossip, which eventually became myth – were intended to expand the affiliation group and annex additional members to it, and are the source of man's pre-eminence over other creatures.

Regardless of their degree of accuracy or truth, life stories and items of gossip are anchored in human consciousness.

The same applies to writing about art, as it evolved from Vasari's *Lives*. In its time, Vasari's book scored tremendous success; in 1568 it was reprinted in a second expanded edition. For later art chroniclers, who wished to make art history a professional discipline in its own right, however, *Lives* was a somewhat awkward reminder of the gap between writing about art and the artists who made it, and in fact, between art and the history of art. While the artists discussed by Vasari – Giotto, Masaccio, Michelangelo, Leonardo, Raphael – continued a grand artistic tradition, Vasari himself was, in some respects, closer to Cimabue, the artist who begins the relay race of the *Lives*: as the chronologically earliest artist in the book, Cimabue is given the aura of a pioneer, but he is also placed the furthest away from the sophistication and mastery of his successors. Later art writers endeavoured to adopt a writing style that would establish both their subjects and themselves as experts in the field, with an aura of professionalism. Focusing on facts, rather than legends, a formal description rather than reliance on dubious biographical details art writing attempted to position itself alongside the exact sciences.

In this sense, as we have already seen, one can ascribe post-modern qualities to Vasari's writing: the rumour and the biographical story as a basis for artistic discussion that is equal in value to any other type of discussion or analysis. One could also describe the lightness with which he shifts from anecdote to historical fact as postmodern fluidity. At the end of the twentieth century, biography re-emerged as a relevant basis for discussion with the appearance of artists whose identity was at the core of their artistic practices.

These are the various 'others' of the art of recent decades. The obscure status of the objects presented by Elmgreen & Dragset – art? mundane objects? collectors' items? museum artifacts? – and of the spaces in which they exhibit – a museum? a house for sale? a ballroom? a fashion accessories shop? – echo the unclear status of the biography that they attempt to present: true or false? Real or concocted? Whose biography is it? The biography of how many? And who are the ones, or the many, behind the life story?

[1] Irit Rogoff, 'Gossip as Testimony. A Postmodern Signature' (1996), in Griselda Pollock (ed.), *Generations and Geographies in the Visual Arts: Feminist Readings*, Routledge, London, 1996, pp.58-65.

[2] Gavin Butt, *Between You and Me: Queer Disclosures in the New York Art World, 1948–1963*, Duke University Press, Durham, NC, 2005.

[3] Yuval Noah Harari, *Sapiens: A Brief History of Humankind*, Random House, New York, 2014.

Whose Biography?

**INTERVIEW BY
GUNNAR B. KVARAN**

GBK: I remember when we first met and I spoke about inviting you to do a retrospective exhibition, you were very sceptical about the idea.

ID: Well, over the past few years, we've been working on more semantic exhibitions, which we've presented in bigger institutions and sometimes in private galleries. Often, the installations take over the whole space and follow one main narrative, building different layers centred around one storyline. When we first came and visited the Astrup Fearnley Museet [ill. 26], it made more sense to us to do something that would be more of a survey show, rather than a retrospective, because the spaces of the museum are very different in scale, very diverse, and we thought that particular environment was not naturally conducive to an overall paradigm exhibition. It seemed to us to be a great challenge and a chance to do something we haven't really done before, which is to combine sculpture, performance, wall pieces *and* room installations – whole environments.

ME: Since we've only been making art for twenty years, not that many curators have invited us to do retrospectives. We were asked once before, and in the end that show was given the title: 'This is the First Day of My Life' (2007, Malmö Konsthall), so it wasn't exactly a retrospective, as you can imagine. In general, we consider every exhibition a new opening to fresh possibilities and that makes it very difficult to make a retrospective. If you look back, it's kind of sad, because it's almost as if you're in a closed room looking back at the door. We prefer to use the works that we've made before and re-introduce them to the audience in a context that gives them a completely new meaning. In that way, they're suddenly placed in new constellations, in new environments that tell new stories. So, in a physical sense, people are experiencing works that have existed before, but in a narrative sense, the works lie about their origins. They put on new masks and pretend to be something other than what they originally were. Exactly like the artists. And therefore, the title 'Biography' has a little ironic twist to it. How do you write a biography? How do you constitute an identity? Will it be your self-image or your image as projected by the work?

GBK: In fact, to do your true retrospective exhibition, one would have to recreate all the exhibitions that you've done in the last twenty years.

ME: There are actually two previous exhibitions included in their entirety in this show. The installation in the cloak-room of the museum is a whole show we did in Madrid, and our closed club *The Mirror* [ill. **20–22**] is an altered version of an exhibition that we did in 2008 in London.

So 'Biography' not only includes a lot of different works from different periods, but also entire shows from earlier on. This is because every time we do an exhibition, we don't consider it as just a collection of artworks, but as an artwork in itself: the exhibition is the work.

GBK: So there's always a total narrative?

ME: Yes.

GBK: But now isn't the moment to do a retrospective, so you've come up with a group of works that are from different periods, and you're presenting them in the space of the Astrup Fearnley Museet as a kind of narrative or narratives. As an introduction, I was wondering if you could describe this narrative of the exhibition and give us some hints concerning the content of the story/stories that are told?

ID: You enter the museum and the first thing you see are crates used to transport artworks: the crates that you're not normally supposed to see, because you always see the works un-crated and installed when you visit a museum. Here, the first welcome is these crates that have crashed together, with semi-destroyed works sticking out here and there. There's something that looks like Jeff Koons' rabbit sculpture sticking out of one of them, and you have a broken Damien Hirst painting in another [ill. 27]. It was painted by an actual assistant of Damien Hirst, so it's a very real fake. [Laughs] These two artists are already very present in the Astrup Fearnley collection and probably still on display in the collection building.

So, there's something destructive in this, but we hope to be constructive in our destructive approach.

ME: And then we pass through a dilapidated gateway [ill. 28] and the next thing we see is a child in a carrycot in front of a cash machine [ill. 45], and a dead man floating face-down in a pool and a big pile of garbage bags coming out of a trash bin. And in the hope of finding some clues to a better life, we climb up the stairs to the first floor in search of enlightenment by some other kind of experience, just to find a whole bunch of small architectural models of museums that all look alike [ill. 31], and on the wall, paintings that consist of actual paint from the walls of powerful international museums, that also appear more or less identical, except for their different shades of white and different textures [ill. 32]…

ID: Again, something you're normally not supposed to see or notice is put on display.

ME: … and in the background you have a real person painting the walls over and over again for absolutely no reason, a Sisyphysian situation [ill. 33]. It's quite embarrassing that the Astrup Fearnley Museum couldn't even finish the exhibition in time! [Laughs] It's a bit like being a bad parent and not having decorated the Christmas tree in time for the children, who come in expecting something wondrous.

GBK: I have the impression that in the basement and on the first floor there's a certain kind of realism, even illusionism, and then upstairs the works are more symbolic, more abstract.

ME: I would say otherworldly.

GBK: Beyond the symbolic world on the second floor and the more realistic world on the first floor, there seem to be different temporalities in the exhibition. When you were working on the installations and the exhibition in general, were you aware of this? Is it intentional or is it a consequence of these different elements coming together?

ME: It's both. I mean, we like the possibilities of combining objects with different histories and meanings. In that way we've always worked in the line of the theory of new materialism: that you can't just look at things from a humanist point of view, and that you can't separate the concept, the textual layer, the spiritual layer, the object, the material. They're not binary oppositions; they all melt together. We work with this in a conscious way, but of course, if you believe in that approach, you also have to expect the unplanned side effect that suddenly happens because the works speak for themselves, beyond our will. They insist on their own lives without us planning that life.

ID: And they're interpreted by many, many different perceptions: people won't see the same things if they come back to see the show a second time. That's something we're always aware of.

GBK: I'd like to explore this notion of the biography: whose biography is it?

ME: Yours. And that of everyone else who comes and looks at it. In this exhibition, the stories we tell are all very closely linked to the difficulties of constituting an identity today. Today, we're artists, we're working class, we're Norwegians, we're gay, in a completely different way from how we were decades ago. We don't identify with our close communities in the same way as we did before. As artists, we can't consider ourselves as something that's avant-garde or outside of society any longer; and as gay men we don't find ourselves living a special lifestyle. So much has changed, and this exhibition shows, through a lot of different fragments, how difficult it is to mix-and-match in order to create an identity in an era dominated by the influences of our digitalised information age, the constant bombardment of news, the random stream of personal information we receive from social media. The issue of identity is present in various shapes throughout the entire show.

GBK: When I compare your plans for the exhibition with many of your other installations, I get the impression that, as the title of the show suggests, it's the story of someone's life. You have the boy, the young man upstairs, and you have the old man – the painter/the worker – and you can easily come to the conclusion that the boy and the old man are the same person. Can you comment on this? Is it your autobiography, or biography? Is the story seen through your eyes or is it from the outside? Is the author within the work or outside the work?

ID: It's impossible for two artists to have an autobiography; it wouldn't make sense to say 'the autobiography of

Elmgreen & Dragset', and this can be a starting point for an answer to this question. Our collaboration is based on dialogue and we've created a third persona, and we know, in a way, who this third person is when we talk to each other, so the 'autobiography' could be something in the head of this non-existent person. That's one thing. The other thing is that these different figures that you see in the exhibition can represent us, or a vision that we have. That doesn't mean that the boy on the fire-escape stairs is Michael Elmgreen or Ingar Dragset, but of course, he is the result of our shared imagination. Even someone like the man floating face-down in the pool can be seen as some sort of a representation of ourselves. The work is called *Death of a Collector* [ill. **15**] and we're not really seen as collectors, that's not really our role in life, but we are part of a world in which collectors play an important role; we're part of the same system or the same culture. We created *Death of a Collector* in order to insert an element of mortality. Death is something one doesn't normally talk much about, but we're all, of course, going to die.

ME: Our shared history in this world can't be written in a linear way; nor can our personal stories be linear. As adults, we have moments where we feel like small children again, and we had moments when we were children when we felt old and mature. The concept of who you are at certain points of time in your life doesn't run along one big line, and the exhibition tries to break up this tendency to aim for linear developments, this naive belief in endless expansion. We have to realise that we can't expand forever – financially, culturally, or in physical terms. One's 'biography' consists of a lot of small, important fragments that might not be chronologically ordered, elements that you can change and move around. It's written according to their urgency at a certain point in time, which will be completely different from what's important in your life at another point. So you don't know if the whole exhibition is happening only inside the head of the boy sitting on the fire-escape stairs, or is the destiny of the baby in front of the cash machine, if it's the last thing you thought of when you were floating face-down in the pool, or if it's what the lady in the swimsuit outside the museum would imagine to be inside that rare building called the Astrup Fearnley Museet.

ID: To talk more about this idea of biography in terms of our art practice in general, you could also say that the exhibition shows elements of the various stages in our collaboration. It starts with performance work and work related to the art institution, the white cube, which is very prevalent in our early work, particularly in the 1990s. For example, you have one person painting the walls every day, over and over again. And we have this huge, impossible towering sculpture of endless white cubes in one corner of the space upstairs, and then we have these extracts of wall paint from famous and important art venues. Somehow the wall paint pieces also have a performative aspect, since this series of white monochromes derives from the labour of a restorer who normally repairs ancient murals and frescos, but who in this instance travelled to all of these contemporary art venues in order to slowly remove layers of their original wall paint, and then applied these samples onto canvases. In the exhibition, we also show more realist works, recognisable sculptures, representations of male figures that deal with the subject of masculinity and vulnerability. And there are works from the period when we did 'The Welfare Show' [ill. 41–46] (2005, Bergen Kunsthall; 2006, Serpentine Gallery), where you could say that the early works, dealing with the white cube as an example of institutional space, took one step further into a world that's maybe easier for a general public to relate to. Here you have a waiting room with a blinking, malfunctioning number display, where you'll never be permitted to see the person you need to talk to, or you have a baby in a carrycot left in front of a cash machine. And finally we show two full-room installations, where you have a number of sub-stories within one setting, like for instance our club installation *The Mirror*, which also incorporates several other works within it. One should also add another entity of works that are predominantly free-standing; in a categorical sense, they're our traditional sculptures that are very rarely shown. This is the first time that we've shown this kind of work in a museum context like this.

ME: But it's fun; it doesn't really matter if it's an installation or an object or a sculpture: it all becomes part of a performance. It's like a stage set where you always feel that an important activity has been going on prior to your arrival, or that something else is just about to happen. There are these indicators that a party has been happening, that someone killed a person who's floating in the pool, that a boy is going to jump down from the fire-escape stairs. You, as the audience, become sort of a private detective, trying to find out what was going on before you arrived at the crime scene.

ID: *The Incidental Self*[1] photographic series probably comes closest to an autobiographical piece. The title says a lot about our perception of identity as a liquid notion. And it's important to note that we started this series in a pre-selfie time. [Laughs]

ME: Other parts of the exhibition deal with the term 'Biography' in a more surreal manner – as kinds of mental images, since our dreams, fears and visions are part of our history as much as our merits and failures. In the middle of a darkened room, which may be the smallest room in the museum, a little bit like a hidden *wunderkammer*, stands a work referring back to early childhood: a cot with a vulture sitting on its edge. Sticking out of the wall nearby is a hand holding a bag of coins. That work is called *Temptation* [ill. 29]. Another piece shows two pairs of hands in a pillow fight [ill. 30]. These works also deal with the classical European sculpture tradition in a way, but they tell very different stories from the grand ones told in art history.

GBK: I had the impression that they were more phantasmagorical.

ME: Yes, they're like dreams, like hallucinations – maybe the hallucinations of the guy in the pool, his last images, or the imaginings of the boy, who's staring at reality but is somewhere else in his mind. It's like when you're in a certain state, in between consciousness and a dream world, and this is what you see. And then you end up in the last room, with a very poetic image of a young man sitting on a stone, looking out the window, dreaming about being a part of the reality that's going on out there in the other world **[ill. 50]**. There's a suggestion of taking more time: maybe we should all waste our time a bit more, dare to give ourselves more opportunities for contemplation and doing nothing. Simultaneously, he's an updated version of the Danish national symbol: the mermaid sitting by the harbour in Copenhagen, always looking as if she's freezing and longing for the love of her life. But she can't have her love because she has a fish tail. However, our young man doesn't have a fish tail – fish tails are out of fashion today. He just has his legs, and actually has the possibility to jump down and embrace what he desires.

ID: We like to use cultural icons and visual clichés as material. There's something in these symbols that touches people emotionally as well as intellectually.

ME: There are whole rooms in the exhibition that have this almost fairy-tale atmosphere. The exhibition takes the shape of strange mental journey from beginning to end. It's a bit like *Hansel and Gretel* when you go through it. At the entrance of the main exhibition hall on the ground floor, visitors have to pass through a little portal, a gate, with a sign board announcing: 'Miracle' **[ill. 28]**. But what you encounter when you walk further into the exhibition is a world that partially indicates personal tragedies, social indignation, and deserted social spaces with the traces of activities that have already happened.

GBK: Do you make reference to other kinds of literature in your work? Because literature – especially the literature of the last hundred years – plays with how you construct narratives.

One can see this very strongly in your installations, especially when it comes to the bigger exhibitions: the narrative structure includes space and time.

ID: We've been inspired narratively and structurally by French literature of the 1960s, like J.M.G. Le Clézio or Georges Perec, but also by a book like Sebastian Faulks' *A Fool's Alphabet* – one of my favourites. I don't love the story itself, but the structure of the book is so great: where you go through the alphabet and find one city or place that relates to each letter and together it makes a wonderful novel. Another example is W.G. Sebald's *The Rings of Saturn*, which presents a number of parallel historical anecdotes and personal experiences. These are examples of references that linger in your mind when you're doing an exhibition like this.

GBK: And is this way of organising narratives in space also connected to your ongoing relationship with the theatre?

ME: Probably it is, in the way that we care about the audience – not who they are and how they'll perceive our work, because everyone's so different and unique, but in the sense that we have an interest in making exhibitions that are for human beings to come and see. So more than just being interested in our own relation to the work or the work in itself, we're interested in the work's afterlife when it leaves our studio and interacts with other humans. And I think that makes it possible to construct these sometimes complex, but at the same time accessible, narratives. They're like visual signs that can be decoded. Even if they're speaking about complicated matters, they can be read.

GBK: Within the narratives in the exhibition, you have these different objects that are made up of very different qualities and materials. We've seen changes in your objects over these last twenty years, from being quite immaterial and neutral to quite spectacular. Can you talk about these changes?

ME: Not only spectacular, but also ugly, scruffy and sometimes even intentionally boring. I think when you're in front of many of our works, the first thing that springs to mind isn't art. If the first thing you think of when you're in front of a work is 'Oh, this is art', then everyone who's not trained in art will back off and feel they're not good enough, or they'll think about the work's worth as art, where it's placed in art history and so on. If the work of art doesn't announce itself as such in the first place, doesn't scream 'Read me as an artwork', but just states 'Listen to what I'm saying', then I think it's possible to imply these narratives in a more complex manner, no matter whether it's an object or something more ephemeral. Because the ephemeral is also material. Just because you can't touch it or can't smell it, doesn't mean it's not there as material.

ID: A lot of influential values today can actually be found in immaterial worlds where you cannot see the *product*, like within big internet companies or financial operations that shift in ways hardly anyone can follow; there are a lot of invisible things that are just as spectacular or powerful as something that's material.

ME: I think it's a big problem to be afraid of material in our world today, because inequality is at the highest it has ever been.

The eighty-three richest people on this planet have a fortune equal to that of half of the world's population. So to me, to turn your back on material and say you don't want to speak about it, is an extreme form of escapism. It's also important for us to find a new dignity for our physical bodies. These brains that we run around with aren't free-floating yet. We're burdened with our bodies but they're excluded most of the time because they're no longer worth anything in terms of labour; they're only used as kitschy sex symbols in advertisements to sell products. We sit in front of our two-dimensional realities, our screens, and our bodies are completely excluded. Only space for our minds remains. And I think part of the new popularity of contemporary art exhibitions is that they're places where people can actually meet in 3-D and socialise in a physical sense. The art space has become a place to celebrate and find new purposes for this construction that is the body – the body confronted with other materialities.

GBK: When I enter 'Biography', I have, maybe for the first time in your exhibitions, a real sense of drama. There's a certain kind of devastation or destruction in the show that I haven't really seen in your work. There are scenes of destruction: the crates in the entrance, the drowning man, leftovers in the nightclub. Is this intentional?

ID: It's true that it's not a very optimistic show; it's more melancholic, with a certain sadness, a certain sense of destruction. Maybe that's where we are at the moment. But we have talked about these things in several shows before, from 'The Welfare Show' to 'Tomorrow' **[ill. 1–8]** at the

Victoria and Albert Museum (2013–14): the destruction of a European identity, Scandinavian identity, the welfare state. And maybe these ideas are intertwined in this show.

GBK: There's less of the kind of witty irony that you often produce.

ME: We've actually only done a few works that have been humorous, but I think people have written more about our humour because that's been easy to grab on to or mediate, and it's overshadowed all the other works. After all, this show consists of a lot of works that we've already done.

ID: Or maybe it's that the artworks have been considered more humorous when seen in isolation, and then when you see them together it becomes clear – and I'm actually kind of happy about this – that there's this more gloomy and doubtful line in the work. For us, that's always been a more important story than the humorous.

GBK: Let's compare the show here with two of your other shows. First, 'The Collectors', which you did for the Venice Biennale in 2009, where you had the privilege of having two pavilions, the Danish and the Nordic Pavilions, which in a brilliant way you made into domestic environments [ill. 14–19]. It was very realistic and effective. And then we have the V&A show, which was recently on in London. That's also framed by the architecture, but there you have all these different temporalities and different symbolic and realistic values that cohabit the space. The pieces work perfectly together, and the narration seems to be quite coherent.

But in this show here, there's a certain kind of dislocation between the architecture of the museum and your show.

ME: The building is new; it's a different situation. If you want to relate to a building's character and features, it needs to have more history. We never just relate to the physical sense of the building. In the V&A, you can relate to its tradition, its history, its prominence and so on, not just the physical features of the museum and the volume of its collection. In Venice, not only do the pavilions have the size and the look of villas, but the whole Giardini resembles an embassy neighbourhood. It's highly competitive; it's like a bourgeois neighbourhood where everyone wants to have the coolest garden. So that has a history. But the new Astrup Fearnley Museet is still a novice in that way: it's relatively clean and not loaded with history yet.

GBK: It becomes more of a stage. One can see more clearly the different structural elements of the different spaces, different temporalities. In the V&A show, the narrative is absorbed into the whole.

ME: It's hard to wrestle with a 150-year-old institution. It's always going to win.

GBK: In 'Biography' the theatricality is more visible.

ME: Absolutely. And when you work with a whole section of a museum, its different levels, corners and passageways, it's like you get a whole new set of tools. You do something where you have a shift, say, from downstairs to upstairs in order to create that complexity. So it's true, it is different.

GBK: In terms of the theatricality, do the boy, the man in the pool, and then the real woman walking into the room share the same time and space?

ID: Physically they do, of course.

ME: But there are multiple moments and activities going on at the same time. As we said, you have the sense that things have taken place before you arrived and that something will happen right after you've left. And that has to do not only with the presence of human performance, but also with the staging of the space; it has that performativity to it.

ID: These temporalities are ways of questioning change. There's also this one music track in the club installation that plays on repeat. It seems to be asking the question: what is actually changing? Everything and nothing simultaneously? That, we can't answer. We can only pose the questions.

This interview was first published in *Elmgreen & Dragset – Biography*, Astrup Fearnley Museet, Oslo, 2014, pp. 38-47.

[1]In the exhibition this series is represented by *The Brightness of Shady Lives* (2005) / *The Black and White Diary* (2009).

Dramatis Personae

IWONA BLAZWICK

To invent, animate and destroy a human being is the prerogative of novelists and scriptwriters. Yet artists Elmgreen & Dragset have entered this domain to create a cast of characters who are protagonists in the sphere of art. We become immersed in their tragi-comic destinies, finding ourselves in uncanny environments created by the artists within the institutional spaces of art – the gallery, the biennale, the museum, the plinth. In contrast to reading a book, or viewing a screen or stage, in the work of Elmgreen & Dragset we meet their dramatis personae in the flesh and undergo a strange psychic charge. Let us meet the cast.

The Collector

Whether pope, aristocrat or industrialist, patron or pillager, it is the collector around whom works of art have always orbited. At the Venice Biennale in 2009, Elmgreen & Dragset transformed the modernist architecture of the Danish and the Nordic Pavilions into two magnificent residences [ill. 14–19]. One was offered for sale as prime real estate; the second was a potential crime scene.

The troubled family who had occupied the first home, had gone, leaving traces of alienation, violence and irrevocable separation. They also left behind them a remarkable collection of surreal, site-specific works made for their home by a range of contemporary artists. Next door, however, Mr B, was at home. Single, gay, also an owner of a sophisticated collection of contemporary art with a homoerotic accent, he could be seen floating face down in his swimming pool **[ill. 15]**. Wearing a simple white shirt and black trousers, he echoes the supine body of Joe Gillis (William Holden) in the film *Sunset Boulevard* (1950). Billy Wilder's drama features a destitute but talented young writer finding refuge from his debts in the mansion of a delusional silent-screen goddess Norma Desmond (Gloria Swanson), now in her dotage. Gillis becomes part of her entourage, a pampered companion who colludes in her dream of a return to Hollywood. Succumbing to the Faustian pact he has struck, he cannot make his escape, losing his will to create and to consummate his true love. Gillis is shot by his jealous patroness, but Mr B's demise is a mystery. In a beautiful soliloquy imagined for Mr B by the writer Dominic Eichler, there is the suggestion that he has AIDS: 'It is a small mercy that my body, at times lugged around resentfully, is beyond that now. I have a couple of large steel "carrier" sculptures by the Spanish artist Pepe Espaliu. He had himself carted around in them … when he became ill from AIDS.'[1] Has the collector also fooled himself that art will buy immortality? Has he substituted worldly possessions for a fulfilled life?

Apparently oblivious to his fate are a group of buff young men, very much alive and one of whom is stark naked **[ill. 16]**.

Lounging on Italian modernist furniture for our viewing pleasure, they are presented as part of Mr B's collection. Can it really be true that a glorious home full of modern classics, desirable men and cutting-edge art can fail to bring happiness?

Since the hilarious antics of Flaubert's *Bouvard* et *Pécuchet*,[2] the business of collecting has occasioned a century of critiques. The accumulation of objects, indeed a consuming interest in objects themselves, generates criticism in terms that range from the socio-economic (the search for prestige, the object as an asset class), the political (the commodification and annulment of an object's autonomy) and psychological (accumulation offsets mortality). It appears that these analyses are applied almost exclusively to collectors of art rather than, say, to bibliophiles, cineastes, philatelists or collectors of ceramics. It is true that conspicuous consumption, self-aggrandisement, money-laundering, tax-avoidance and speculation are accusations that can all be laid at the feet of some or other art collector. But is this sustained critical vehemence masking something else? What many commentators appear to miss – or perhaps they simply disapprove of it – is the most common characteristic of dedicated collectors of art: their interest in aesthetics.

In their riff on the freebies circulated in international art events (catalogues and goody bags), the *Bag-alogue* compiled by Elmgreen & Dragset for the Venice Biennale contains a fold-out sheet of quotes selected by Anna Echterholter, a cultural theorist from the Humboldt University in Berlin.[3]

She assembles a scattering of critiques of collectors by Jean Baudrillard and Susan Stewart alongside quotes from the definitive representatives of the Aesthete – Charles Baudelaire and Joris-Karl Huysmans. A quote from Baudrillard reveals the problem: 'Any given object can have two functions: it can be utilized, or it can be possessed.' But is that really all?

Mr B confirms the popular view of a collector: wealthy, acquisitive and effete. But Elmgreen & Dragset also subtly undermine this stock characterisation. They echo the strategies of portraitists such as Holbein or Ingres by setting their characters within fully realised interiors where objects can be read as attributes of their subject. Looking around the house of Mr B, we find Wolfgang Tillmans' insouciant scene of naked, tumescent young men dozing on a picnic rug; and a display case throbbing with Tom of Finland's drawings of hyper-phallic gay bikers and strutting officers. A countercultural icon, Tom of Finland made work that embraced many taboos, including fetishising Nazis. But as he himself remarked, 'In my drawings I have no political statements to make, no ideology. I am thinking only about the picture itself. The whole Nazi philosophy, the racism and all that, is hateful to me, but of course I drew them anyway – they had the sexiest uniforms!'[4]

The artists have composed a letter from Mr B to a lover in Berlin, published as an edition for the magazine, *Texte zur Kunst* in 2009. He writes, 'I'm really so foolishly pleased with such vast extents of art that I'm falling into a bottomless pit of delight.' It is not clear whether his death is murder, suicide or accident – perhaps he just had a heart attack.

Possibly his tragi-comic demise is also a question for us, the bystanders and the critics: this accumulator of objects, this unapologetic pleasure-seeker – ask yourself, do you feel that these are his just deserts?

To return to Baudrillard's assertion about a dual relationship with the object – utility or possession – Mr B knows better. He knows that the art object can be intellectually and sensually enthralling. He knows also that art can offer a form of identification. Mr B's collection represents a sexual identity. In the context of a home, it becomes domesticated, normal. In the context of a state-endorsed world summit of national cultures, it becomes transgressive.

Mr B turns up again, only his feet visible, in a mortician's cabinet. It is 2011 and Elmgreen & Dragset have transformed the Galerie Emmanuel Perrotin into a morgue [ill. 24]. The dead collector has found immortality by becoming a work of art. Creating a theatre in the round, Elmgreen & Dragset dissolve the fourth wall, enabling us to nose around, to read the clues for evidence that takes us beyond the categorical stereotypes – Gay Single Man/ Art Collector – to search for more slippery, ambivalent and multi-perspectival truths.

The Architect

The figure of the architect has become a defining cultural icon of modernity. The charisma attributed to visionaries such as Frank Lloyd Wright and his Prairie School, or Le Corbusier and his sky-bound designs for urban transformation in the first half of the twentieth century found a mid-century fictional equivalent in the character of Howard Roark, the architect hero of Ayn Rand's 1943 bestseller, *The Fountainhead*. This Neitzschean modernist refuses to compromise his progressive architectural vision to the forces of tradition or collectivism.

By contrast with the figure of the uncompromising genius set to transform society through construction, Elmgreen & Dragset created an architect who has never built anything and is literally invisible. We can, however, hear him taking a shower in his grand yet shabby apartment on the third floor of the Victoria and Albert Museum [ill. 2–8].[5] Even before we read the film script in the booklet [ill. 1] that accompanies the exhibition, we know that Norman Swann is the scion of a wealthy family.[6] His rooms are adorned with inherited masterpieces, or at least the dark squares on the wallpaper where they once hung before being discretely sold off. He is a smoker and a drinker. He is clearly broke. But he is also a utopian. His sequence of rooms boasts a library and an impressive collection of ornaments ranging from a priceless Ming vase to a mass-produced Art Deco porcelain ashtray adorned with a naked boy, to a poster from an exhibition held at the Whitechapel Gallery in 1956 called 'This is Tomorrow'. We can see that our homes are like archaeological sites, where the artefacts of different cultural and social periods exist in the same space, brought together by one life.

There are two unexpected rooms. The first is a small studio where we find architectural drawings, statements and models for public housing that testify to Swann's ambition to improve society, to frame a better future [ill. 5–6]. The style of building he envisages reflects the influence of a generation of architects working in Britain in the 1960s, such as Archigram or Cedric Price, with their emphasis on flexible spaces, modules and mobility – Swann has designed houses on stilts, literally 'castles in the air'. It becomes clear that none have ever been built. Perhaps he felt guilt about his privileged background. Swann dreams of helping the many, not just the individual. The impossibly utopian nature of his housing designs and his innate inability to bring his vision to fruition combine to produce stasis. For all his dreams of a better tomorrow, the past is all around him, an inescapable burden. Perched above his models and drawings is a stuffed vulture, a presentiment of doom. The second surprise is presented by an incongruously modish kitchen, brand new, expensive and completely out of character with the fading gentility of the rest of the apartment [ill. 7].

The inner life of Norman Swann is hinted at through the script in the booklet. We discover that he taught architecture. The script sets him in a late-night confrontation with a former student, Daniel, a rising star of interior design whose clients are celebrities. He has bought Swann's apartment and it is he who has installed the vulgar new kitchen. It is hinted that he exchanged sexual favours for academic preferment; his acquisition of the flat is an Oedipal act of revenge. Norman may have seduced him, but he has also allowed Daniel to disguise his mediocrity.

The architect's name suggests a conflation of two sources, one literary and the other architectural. In *Swann's Way*, the first volume of Marcel Proust's *In Search of Lost Time* the narrator comes to the realisation that Charles Swann, a family friend, leads an unknowable existence outside his relationship with his circle. The narrator comes to understand that identity is not fixed and conferred by birth into a social caste, as his family imagines; rather, it is flexible, continually being reshaped. 'Our social personality', the narrator remarks, 'is a creation of the minds of others.'[7]

The other reference, at least in the mind of a UK visitor, is to the architect Norman Foster, whose steel-and-glass functionalism can be encountered in cities around the world. The composite Norman Swann upends Ayn Rand's uncompromising genius figure. Just as his possessions are drawn from the holdings of the V&A and reinserted into their original domestic setting, so the figure of the architect is reunited with a lived reality of fallibility, compromise and unfulfilled yearning for the utopian possibilities of design. We have only to look at the disparity between the 'Radiant Cities' dreamed of by Corbusier and the realities of high-rise social housing to be thankful that his utopias remained unrealised. In their monograph of 2008, the artists quote the French writer, Georges Perec: 'All utopias are depressing because they leave no room for chance, for difference, for the "miscellaneous". Everything has been set in order and order reigns. Behind every utopia there is always some great taxonomic design: a place for each thing and each thing in its place.'[8]

The Muse

Did Mr B or Norman Swann ever look up the handsome Andrea Candela [ill. 23] on GayRomeo, 'Europe's biggest online chat and dating community'? This fresh-faced young man with his charmingly tousled hair, ripe lips and dark brown, faraway eyes, is a composite of all the most desirable qualities sought by users of GayRomeo. Candela has made several appearances – his debut, in the form of two photographs, was at the Massimo di Carlo gallery in Milan in 2006; he made another tantalising appearance at the Malmö Konsthall in 2007. Alongside details of his physique and username 'juniorboyz', he submits his profile on GayRomeo simply as 'new in Berlin. I don't speak German!'

Andrea Candela is arranged in the manner of a classical nude, but wears a hooded sweatshirt, loose jeans and sneakers. Where Ingres' Odalisque has her divan and Manet's Olympia her couch, this young man is lying, variously, on a white rug, a mattress on the floor, and a crumpled trestle bed. These 'soft plinths' are less about display than about communicating Candela's way of life – they signify the carefree existence of a student, possibly couch-surfing or living in a hostel. His pose is unselfconscious and meditative. Although he is lying down, his loose, casual clothing and dreamy self-containment bespeak a pubescent innocence far from the sexually provocative poses of pornography. His few possessions – an electric guitar, laptop and football in one scenario, a candle, books and papers in another – combine with the cell-like austerity of his surroundings to communicate a lack of funds and a freewheeling lifestyle, a young life in transition.

Whatever our sexuality, we cannot help but be seduced by this tender character. Both feminine and masculine, he also embodies a state between innocence and experience. We are given access to his private space as voyeurs, but he remains compellingly remote. Freud remarked that it is because children exclude us from their own imaginative worlds that they exert a fascination for us. Candela also suggests a Rousseauian naturalism, uncorrupted by socialisation and adulthood. His very surname is the scientific definition for 'a unit of luminous intensity'. He draws our gaze like moths to a flame.

Despite his innocent demeanour, however, he has made himself sexually available. Elmgreen & Dragset let us see the flurry of excited proposals that his posting has elicited. 'Wow you look very sweet' or 'Prettiest thing in life I've ever seen.' Alongside 'when can we suck and fuck', and offers of 'pocket money' for sex, some gay Romeos express wistful longing, particularly the older men: 'I am 38 years old and I hope that is not to old for you … I miss a man I can love and I get love from.'[9]

Andrea Candela is made of wax, but like Coppelia or Frankenstein, he has been animated by his creators. His life lies in the desire of others. He is a muse. He may inspire the sexual fantasy of deflowering a virgin; perhaps of being possessed and moulded like an acolyte; perhaps just possessing a love object. Candela is also the vehicle for dreams of freedom from the burdens of responsibility. He recalls the luminous Tadzio in Visconti's film *Death in Venice* (1981).

This adolescent son of a Polish countess has caught the eye of Gustav von Aschenbach, an aging composer played by Dirk Bogarde, who is also succumbing to cholera. As the hair dye used to disguise his age trickles down von Aschenbach's sweating temples, he looks out to sea where Tadzio stands against the setting sun, arm extended towards him. Beautiful but unattainable, Candela is the obscure object of desire; but as a kind of democratic composite of most sought-after characteristics, is he also a portrait of male desire and a wished-for self image?

The Maid

Unlike Mr B or Norman Swann or even Andrea Candela, Rosa [ill. 47] has no possessions and no room of her own. She has been in attendance at several of Elmgreen & Dragset's mise-en-scenes – the stoic voiceless presence of the servant. Rosa is not realised naturalistically, but cast in gold like a statue. Although the artists are using the vocabulary of ancient figures or monuments to give her a totemic presence, the dignity of this figure is undercut by her uniform. Her status is signalled by her white lace headpiece, tied with a black ribbon behind her hair. Her dress is an unflattering cut, in a practical black. The protective apron also signifies that she will be carrying food or liquids, or maybe cleaning. Her shoes are designed for comfort, since she will be required to stand for long periods – paired with white ankle socks, they are also slightly infantile. She holds her arms behind her back in a gesture of subservient attention.

Rosa's uniform is instantly recognisable to us, in part because of a proliferation of books, films and period dramatisations about the life 'below stairs' of domestic servants such as the television series *Downton Abbey*. What is discomfiting, however, is that neither her outfit nor her stance look out of place today. Rosa and her golden sisters in servitude – Irina, Tala and others cast by the artists from immigrant women according to the location of the exhibition in which they appear – are part of a new underclass. They are not domestic servants as a result of the hierarchies of a native class system; rather they have the subaltern status of the global economic migrant exiled by the extremes of third-world poverty. In 2010, two of these maids appeared at a party that we glimpsed in silhouette (but were not invited to) in Elmgreen & Dragset's exhibition at the ZKM Museum in Karlsruhe **[ill. 12]**. It is probably an art-world event, but could equally be a film premiere or concert after-party. For all the radical ambitions of creative practitioners and the communities we form around them, we collectively fail to notice who is serving our drinks.

The Children

Despite being a mainstay of religious painting from Byzantium until the mid-twentieth century, children have for the most part disappeared from contemporary art (with notable exceptions including the Chapman Brothers' pornographic child mannequins and Charles Ray's naked family sculpture). They can be tricky as subject matter, prone to misinterpretation in terms ranging from sentimentality to paedophilia. Elmgreen & Dragset have risked entering this terrain, adding a series of boys and a baby to their cast.

The most exuberant is the golden boy who rocked on his horse in one of the world's most prominent public spaces – the Fourth Plinth in London's Trafalgar Square **[ill. 49]**. Wearing just a pair of shorts, he is barefoot and bare-chested. Naturalistically sculpted, he raises one arm and leans back on his 'IKEA style toy horse'. Speaking about his genesis, Elmgreen comments, 'We've spent a whole year in production, from making the first model to the moulds and finally having the bronze poured in. Then, when we scaled it up we found this cute little boy had lost his fragility and turned into a fucking monster!'[10] Indeed, his seamless perfection has something kitsch, even fascistic, about it. Metaphorically the boy rocks between the innocent sword-and-sorcery fantasies of childhood and the triumphalist militarism embodied by his fellow statues in the square – Horatio Nelson occupies centre stage and is flanked by a host of other admirals and generals. They and the boy are in many senses anachronisms. As Dragset added in the same interview, 'we made him in an old-fashioned, nostalgic style, not only so he could blend into the square, but because kids nowadays don't have rocking horses – they play war games to get their thrills. So it's also a memorial for toys and fantasy.' The warriors who surround him have for the most part been forgotten, their victories recounted in history books that are now up for revision – if, that is, they are even retrieved from the library shelves. For the so-called 'tablet generation', even the library is a thing of the past. This huge and exuberant child is whooping and waving from another era of representation that disappears a little with each generation. The nascent warrior now takes a virtual form, slashing and burning through the levels of a computer game; the wars and the violence will continue.

Another, sadder boy appeared at the ZKM party where Rosa was serving. He could also be spotted in Norman Swann's fireplace. Wearing a grey serge uniform with maroon piping around the sleeves and a crest on his cap, the schoolboy – perhaps it is the young Norman – has drawn his knees up to his pale, thoughtful face [ill. 4]. By contrast with his bronze counterpart, he huddles into himself, his crossed hands clasped in front of his legs, his shoulders hunched. The huge ceremonial marble fireplace, devoid of a fire, is the boy's space of retreat. He has been given an expensive education, but perhaps little else. He has no playmates and the grown-ups appear to have forgotten about him. Standing on the mantelpiece is a porcelain figure riding a stallion; hanging above is the boy's portrait, disproportionately large. His expression remains withdrawn and timorous. Society has great ex-pectations that will, as with Pip and Estella in Charles Dickens' story, distort or repress natural freedoms.[11] For Elmgreen & Dragset this narrative relates most specifically to the free expression of sexual identity.

The loss of innocence is traced right back to infancy. A pram has bright plastic teething toys spelling out H O M O. An exquisitely attired baby in a carry cot has appeared in a range of locations – the back of a car surrounded by gallery guides and receipts for luxury goods; and at the base of a cash machine [ill. 45]. The baby is clean, beautifully dressed and sleeping soundly. Nonetheless it has been forgotten. Its parents are busy looking for their heart's desire among inanimate objects.

Elmgreen & Dragset's visual theatre spans life and death. There are other less prominent roles – Tanya, the Gallerist, sleek in high heels yet distraught over the delivery of a damaged crate; waxwork patients in hospital beds; live security guards and gallery painter-decorators, all performing institutional rituals on the art-world stage [ill. **48, 42, 43, 33**]. They are ciphers that chime with Boccaccio, Chaucer or Hogarth, characters from cautionary tales. Yet the artists also give their dramatis personae poignant and revelatory twists. Their genius lies in how they stage our encounter with their uncanny doppelgangers.

'In telling a story, one of the most successful devices for easily creating uncanny effects is to leave the reader in uncertainty whether a particular figure in the story is a human being or an automaton.'[12] To encounter a wax figure or mannequin is to undergo a moment of psychic disturbance; our anthropomorphising instincts seek to recognise the human. Our senses disagree. In the work of Elmgreen & Dragset, further disorientation is caused by the precision with which the artists create entire environments that are then transposed into the wrong contexts. To enter an occupied, slightly shabby apartment, complete with cigar butts and a leaking ceiling in the midst of the climate-controlled display spaces of the museum, for example, is to experience cognitive dissonance. The double-take occasioned by these encounters opens a lacuna, a momentary rupture in the veil of our perception. It is through this lacuna that Elmgreen & Dragset introduce new ways of understanding art, love and the politics of social engagement.

1 Dominic Eichler, 'Another Death in Venice', in Peter Weibel and Andreas F. Beitin (ed.), *Elmgreen & Dragset: Trilogy*, Thames & Hudson, London/ZKM, Karlsruhe, 2011, pp.269, 272.

2 Gustave Flaubert, *Bouvard* et *Pécuchet*, 1881.

3 Elmgreen & Dragset, *The Collectors: Bag-alogue*, The Danish and Nordic Pavilions, 53rd Venice Biennale, 2009.

4 Quoted by F. Valentine Hooven (1993), *His Life and Times*, St. Martins Press, New York, p.30; Tom of Finland, Wikipedia entry.

5 Elmgreen & Dragset, 'Tomorrow', installation at the Victoria and Albert Museum, London, October 2013 – January 2014.

6 Elmgreen & Dragset, *Tomorrow: Scenes from an unrealised film*, Victoria and Albert Museum, London, 2013.

7 Lydia Davis, introduction, Marcel Proust, *In Search of Lost Time*, trans. Lydia Davis, Penguin Classics, London, 2004.

8 Georges Perec, 'Utopias', quoted in *Elmgreen & Dragset: This is the First Day of My Life*, Hatje Cantz Verlag, Ostfildern, 2008, p.242.

9 GayRomeo postings, ibid., pp.48–9.

10 Interview with Ossian Ward, *Time Out*, online listings magazine, London, February, 2012.

11 Charles Dickens, *Great Expectations*, 1872–74.

12 Ernst Jentsch, *On the Psychology of the Uncanny*, 1906, trans. Roy Sellars, 1995.

Is there a master in this house at all?
Reflections on Elmgreen & Dragset's
'Biography' at Astrup Fearnley
Museet, spring 2014

SUSANNE CHRISTENSEN

t is Saturday night, it is late November, and I am trudging through the snow down Aker Brygge, Oslo. The sky and the sea are dark, silent forms on the periphery of my vision, but on the wharf everything is glittering in a scintillating array of colour. A group of people are in the final stages of a drunken office Christmas party; there is much tottering on sky-high stilettos and animal roaring from well-dressed young people with obviously impaired balance. At the outermost point of the wharf – on Tjuvholmen – is Astrup Fearnley's new Renzo Piano building [ill. 26]. Viewed from Aker Brygge it looks like a self-effacing triangle seeking to mediate between the flat, expansive plane formed by the sea and the strip of high-end shops and restaurants. I stomp around the museum building, noting with a taut smile how the deliciously stylish architectural lines communicate with the faraway, almost blurred profile of the mountains beyond.

In the early 2000s I was very familiar with Astrup Fearnley's permanent collection of works by artists including Jeff Koons and Damien Hirst. The museum's former location in Kvadraturen, a grid established by King Christian IV after a disastrous fire in 1624 and located just a few minutes from Oslo Sentralstasjon, was very comfortable and convenient; the museum acted as a well-heated waiting room when I travelled by train and bus between Bergen and Copenhagen. I had a particularly close and cosy relationship with Hirst's cow and calf in formaldehyde, *Mother and Child (Divided)* (1993), which was placed at the furthest point of the room, allowing rays of light to shimmer and play between the glass panes.

Here at the new building, it seems as if the lively crowd scenes out on Aker Brygge are penetrating the space; the walls are not resistant. Many of the spaces in the Danish-Norwegian duo Elmgreen & Dragset's exhibition 'Biography', a show that places their work in new contexts and can be experienced as a huge stage set, do not stand apart from the culture of entertainment and hedonistic pleasure that lives outside the museum. As is the case in any game of power, there is a tension between the high and the low; this can be felt in quite concrete terms as you pass through the doors leading into 'Biography'. On top of a seemingly unstable structure made from crates, a copy of one of Jeff Koons' inflatable silver rabbits pokes out its ears [ill. **27**]. At the bottom, in the wardrobe section, mundane activities are taking place [ill. **25**]. At the top of the wall is a fire escape like those in New York; here, a powerless boy is gazing at a once-powerful man floating face down in a swimming pool.

There are moments of disorientation and sudden insight. Illusions leak and crack, and desire and confusion turn my experience of the rooms upside down. Their design and layout do not conjure up a purely imaginative world; rather, the works repeatedly and insistently call my attention to the coarse, crude way in which worlds have been stitched together. We *are* linked, but there is no escaping the seasickness, and no way of getting out of doing a certain amount of thinking yourself.

In many cities, very notably Bergen, the art space is facing increasing competition with the urban space. For example, Bergen's Festivalplassen square with its view of Ulriken has, in a relatively short time, grown into a veritable orgy of appealing architectural lines and colours that communicate with the mountains. Here, you pass from one carefully thought-out stage set to the next. Exhibitions of contemporary art quite often take the form of total installation; examples that spring to mind include those by the German artist Carsten Höller, Børre Sæthre's sci-fi-inspired exhibition at Bergen Kunsthal in 2007, and Knut Åsdam's show in the same space in 2010, where a labyrinth of metal fences made the indoor rooms seem like outdoor spaces. The crowds of people are like molten, glowing, liquid glass being poured through the spaces. How are we being shaped? And to what purpose? Are we being moulded to freedom and struggle, or to shopping and endless pleasure? Is there even a conflict between the two?

The museum, however, insists on one's participation to a greater extent than a furniture showroom, for example, which wishes to sell a picture of a perfect world. But even the furniture showrooms of today are dreaming post-utopian dreams. Once – it must have been back in the 1970s, in a suburb of Copenhagen – my father and I walked through the showrooms of IKEA. Quite typically, the various rooms took the form of potential realities: little family utopias that you could step into and out of, trying them on for size. IKEA's world was sensuous and colourful, full of soft fabrics and smooth, glossy surfaces. *Do I want to live here? Do we want to live here, dad?* The rooms offered promises of an ideal Nordic family life. There was no suffering or want here, there was no loneliness, and perhaps there were no possible ways of arranging one's life other than along the path offered by the heterosexual nuclear family. After all, at that time IKEA's furniture showrooms were infused by ideas about an active, social life – a *vibrant, lived* life. Now, the popular Scandinavian furniture shop seems to be undergoing a paradigm shift, or it may be more accurate to say that it is *humanity* that is undergoing a paradigm shift, and the furniture store is merely reflecting this trend. In the IKEA store in Berlin-Tempelhof, the rooms now look like luxurious burial chambers. After the store began selling flat-screen televisions, the rooms changed in honour of the screens on the wall. Everywhere, the sofas – which are practically beds – point towards the screens. What is this, Plato's cave? Lifestyle turned deathstyle? Must we get used to the fact that it is impossible to go outside due to drone wars and natural disasters?

Elmgreen & Dragset have come a long way from the vibrant 1990s art scene of Copenhagen, where Dane Michael Elmgreen and Norwegian Ingar Dragset met and became partners in art (and, for the first ten years, romantically too), to the international circuits in which they move today. Associations with other famous artist duos such as the Anglo-Italian Gilbert & George and Pierre et Gilles from France spring readily to mind, but to me even more names present themselves, such as Marina Abramović and Ulay (in their early work Elmgreen & Dragset also worked with performance art, a genre that can easily cross the divide between art and life), as well as the star-crossed lovers Romeo and Juliet. Elmgreen & Dragset, however, have not built their life's work on a story of tragic, forbidden love; rather, they have based it on more fundamental questions pertaining to desire, power and how our surroundings shape us. In 2011, talking to Canadian sociologist Sarah Thornton, Elmgreen commented: 'Our initial ambition was to express our worldview more publicly. It was not so much that we thought we were special. It was about a lack. We missed seeing our perception of the world represented.' Later in the same interview Dragset says: 'There's a lot of love in our work.' Instead of being consigned to a secret boudoir, love becomes part of their work. Intoxicated by sheer happiness, couples in love often feel as if they are the centre of the world, but given that the world is full to overflowing with stories about heterosexual love, the space allowed for other kinds of narrative can seem limited in scope – relegated and squeezed into bars and techno clubs rather than gushing forth in an unselfconscious flow though public spaces.

We like to think of the world as being one, as a unity, and indeed it can often feel that way, but there are bumps in the road, as if various different worlds – your world, my world, the art world, the 'real world' and the queer world – have been poorly stitched together. There are moments of disorientation and sudden insight. The doors between these worlds are not necessarily functional. There may be transparent walls in what we thought were perfectly ordinary, gender-segregated toilets, and the discharge pipe from a urinal may wind pointlessly across the floor like a dangerous snake, connecting itself to other urinals in surprising ways **[ill. 58]**. *Please, where is the master bedroom? Is there a master in this house at all?*

In the 1990s, the time when the duo began their collaboration, queer theory formulated a critique of identity politics and a heavy-handed storming of universally held values – the laws of the white, straight male, of simplified opposites and a perception of power as a kind of absolute monarchy: *Come on, let's storm the palace gates and rule!* Conceptual art keeps the game rather more open-ended, inviting audiences to form their own experiences and opinions. Is the white cube too pure for political protest? Is it the right place for a demonstration where people carry signs bearing simple statements? Possibly not, but even so there is nothing exalted about Elmgreen & Dragset's artistic practice. Their use of the gallery space does not shut out the sounds of the mundane world; rather, they repeatedly challenge the notion of the neutral gallery space by means of both subtle and brutal displacements: they have buried it **[ill. 40]**, torn down its walls, transformed it into a shop and moved it to a desert.

The goodie bag handed out to visitors to the Elmgreen &
Dragset-curated exhibition 'The Collectors' at the 53rd
Venice Biennale in 2009 (the term should be taken quite
literally; the bag contained many small press objects produced by various artists, but also a delicious, fully edible
sausage) included a small white die. The duo have worked in
Neukölln in Berlin since the 1990s, and so they presumably
know that the gallery space, the white cube, is known as
weißer Würfel in Germany. A *Würfel* is, strictly speaking, a
die of the kind used for gambling, not a cube in the sense
of a space that may be entered. Context has become an art
object in its own right, as the art critic Brian O'Doherty
states in his seminal essay 'Inside the White Cube: Ideologies
of the Gallery Space',[1] and perhaps that is why 'cube'
becomes 'die' in Elmgreen & Dragset's many games with
the cathedral-like purity of the gallery space. According
to O'Doherty the gallery space – the supposed neutrality
of which arose to contain the essentially timeless modernist
art of the twentieth century – was 'constructed along laws
as rigorous as those for building a medieval church'. The
ruling class could retain its grip on the masses by appearing
to have a special compact with this ritual space, purged
of all mundane noise and turmoil. Power and authority
could claim a connection to the divine through this space,
where abstract forms glide serenely along in an aloof, exalted
manner, liberated from all bodily filth and human diversity.
The notion of a neutral gallery space is part of a power
structure, and the duo have worked with this fact in the
series *Powerless Structures*, an array of symbolic displacements
of power, including a circular bar where the beer taps
face the customer/audience; a short-circuiting of sorts.

What happens when the iconic spaces of the gay subculture – such as the sauna and the disco – are suddenly relocated to the museum in all their overwhelming specificity? This is surely not a church, right? It certainly isn't *my* church – *sorry, I don't pray that way!*

'We missed seeing our perception of the world represented', said Elmgreen in that interview with Thornton. The German philosopher Edmund Husserl (1859–1938) inscribes himself in history as the founder of modern phenomenology. The British-Pakistani theorist Sara Ahmed takes Husserl's work as her point of departure in her book *Queer Phenomenology. Orientations, Objects, Others,*[2] where the issues addressed include how we navigate and orient ourselves in space. Our sexual orientation, too, is described in spatial terms: what do we point ourselves towards – or, more accurately, what are we called upon to point towards? To 'give directions' means to show the way, but also to teach, to direct. There is often a point A and a point B and a straight line between them – *please get straight to the point.* Our genealogy is also ordered in lines as straight as possible: we are called upon to reproduce inherited traditions, things that are passed down to us. Ahmed draws on her own experience as a lesbian when she says that: 'The lesbian body does not extend the shape of this world, as a world organized around the form of the heterosexual couple. Inhabiting a body that is not extended by the skin of the social means the world acquires a new shape and makes new impressions.' A displacement – or at worst an exclusion – takes place, but this can be turned into a creative potential. The Swedish theorist Katarina Bonnevier's *Behind Straight Curtains.*

Towards a Queer Feminist Theory of Architecture studies historical examples of queer architecture.[3] The Swedish writer Selma Lagerlöf's property Mårbacka in Värmland, which she redesigned after winning the Nobel Prize for Literature in 1909, and the architect and designer Eileen Gray's house E.1027 on the French Riviera, created during the years from 1926 to 1929, both constitute groundbreaking works within the construction of sensuous utopias with a queer sensibility.

In 'Biography' we once again come across the tragic art collector Mr B; as at the 2009 Venice Biennale, he is shown here floating face-down in his swimming pool, a victim of an art-loving, hedonistic lifestyle. One of the most surprising special devices in Mr B's home was a central bathroom with glass walls [ill. 14]. Large tree trunks shot up through the floor, and the drainpipe from the sink turned and twisted like a silver snake. We are used to bathroom plumbing and pipes designed in as rational a fashion as possible; the water should be transported from point A to point B in the straightest line available, but here it has run amuck to invent new, wild shapes for itself. The master of the house may have perished, but the current exhibition is a narrative about life as it is lived, a biography of the artists' lives through all their works of art from the 1990s onwards. But perhaps it is also the biography of your own vibrant, tremulous, unruly life as you pass through the exhibition.

I myself have passed through 'Biography' countless times – in front of my computer, while taking a shower, and in the minutes before I drift off to sleep. I have visualised the exhibition on the basis of the plans laid by the artists in co-operation with the museum in the early days of 2014. Which parts of the exhibition was I unable to predict? First of all, the work that is everywhere in the air, more or less prominently: the audio track looping in the nightclub *The Mirror* [ill. **20–22**]. The song *Too Late* evokes and accentuates a melancholy atmosphere, a sense of loss that is an inherent feature of the works and is accentuated by the more or less remote *Twin Peaks*-like piece of 1980s electro-pop. What am I grieving for? I feel a certain connection with the artists insofar as we belong to the same generation; at any rate Ingar Dragset and I were born in the same year. Did we both hit the dance floor around the same time in the 1980s? The narrative of sexual identity is often identified as a time of experimentation until you find your particular shelf and settle there. After that, there are no uncertainties left; you are fully finished, as it were. Sexual identity is defined through confrontations with its opposite; we think of it as youthful messing about. The unfinished self is bouncing off the sound of melancholy 1980s electro-pop. It becomes lost, disappears and drowns in a state of gender-transcending euphoria.

Still, the grief is so deep and so profound that it goes beyond the personal stories of Dragset or myself. Is this a universal feeling? I feel that the sense of sadness that fills me is also about cultural repression. The 1980s atmosphere is accentuated further by the work *Amigos* from 2011 [ill. **25**]. Two Greek gods deriving from the cradle of Western civilisation are posing behind a pink neon sign forming the word *Amigos*.

They are friends, or 'friends' – they are lovers really, and they have been lovers since Western civilisation first arose. The illegal love – for which I am too late – is documented in the personal snapshot series 'The Incidental Self' with the works *The Brightness of Shady Lives* (2005) and *The Black and White Diary* (2009), the jolliest entry here, even if it does take on a somewhat *altmodisch* quality due to the fireplace-like framing. But why am I seized by a sense of sadness? In her book *Gender Trouble: Feminism and the Subversion of Identity*, Judith Butler writes that 'heterosexual melancholy is culturally instituted as the price of stable gender identities'[4] and goes on to say that the idea of homosexuality is required in order for heterosexuality to remain stable. Homosexuality becomes forbidden, but is still necessary within the cultural framework.

I step quietly through the rooms; the soundtrack susurrates in the air and makes something rise up in me, a kind of wave. In this sense, the museum *is* a kind of church, a public space where we can be overwhelmed by melancholia and grief, but this church is not a white space outside of time.

[1] First published in *Artforum* in 1976.

[2] Duke University Press, Durham, NC, 2006.

[3] Axl Books, Stockholm, 2007.

[4] Routledge, New York, 1990, p.70.

Tomorrow is Here

MARTIN HERBERT

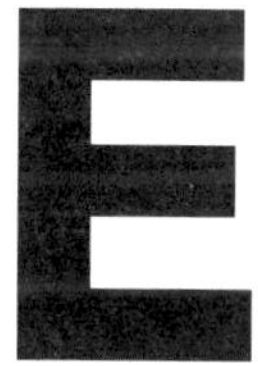ven if you're only a casual observer of contemporary art, chances are you've seen Michael Elmgreen and Ingar Dragset's work. Perhaps you haven't trekked to Texas to witness *Prada Marfa* (2005), a fully stocked, permanently closed Prada store erected near the desert town associated with that pioneer of Minimalism, Donald Judd. Maybe you missed *Drama Queens*, their 2007 play at London's Old Vic featuring seven remote-controlled sculptures bitching volubly about being stuck in a museum, voiced by the likes of Kevin Spacey and Jeremy Irons [ill. 51]. And you may not have caught 'The Collectors' (2009), the Danish and Nordic Pavilions of the 53rd Venice Biennale converted into mimicries of art collectors' homes [ill. 14–19]. Still, if you crossed Trafalgar Square in the eighteen months leading up to last April, you probably noted *Powerless Structures, Fig. 101* (2012), the Danish/Norwegian artists' incongruous bronze statue of a child on a rocking horse, itself riding the fourth plinth [ill. 49].

This, admittedly, was a fairly modest example of the merry havoc the duo have played with conventions of display, and the contemporary art world's protective self-seriousness, since the mid-1990s. But *Fig. 101* still exemplifies Elmgreen & Dragset's ability to fuse provocation and humour with a sociological intelligence that addresses the wider world too. Clearly the carefree kid was no conquering hero and the statue didn't celebrate authoritarianism and grandiosity, though it amplified them in the figures around it. It also insinuated how citizens of the West are increasingly trained, from an early age, to see being celebrated as a meaningful aim and to 'sell' themselves as fascinating personalities. (The rocking horse, mixing antiquated and modern contours, evokes nostalgia for a pre-social-media age.) *Fig. 101* constituted, furthermore, a mischievous suggestion from non-natives that the UK might lean less on former glories and consider future generations instead.

In terms of public exposure, this is a long way from Elmgreen & Dragset's earliest works, Sisyphean gallery performances such as *Untitled* (1996), in which the pair knitted, then unravelled a 100-metre piece of white cloth, and which were followed by the 100-plus *Powerless Structures* artworks that have become their central project. Beginning in 1997, this series initially positioned the gallery space as embodying authority – able to make anything within its white walls seem meaningful – and transgressed it by offering up deliberately short-circuiting, futile, seemingly jokey proposals. *Powerless Structures, Fig. 2*, from that year, involved paint tins with circular pools of paint next to them, in mismatched colours, while *Twelve Hours of White Paint/Powerless Structures, Fig. 15* (also 1997) saw a white cube space alternately whitewashed and rinsed clean by the artists for a dozen hours straight.

Powerless Structures, Fig. 69 (1999), in Melbourne, simulated a stack of white paper flying out of a window; *Powerless Structures, Fig. 162* (2001) comprised a tipped-over plinth with a broken green vase lying next to it.

By 2003 Elmgreen & Dragset were deconstructing galleries literally. For *Spaced Out* they removed the walls of Portikus Frankfurt, leaving only the floor, skylight and roof, supported by pillars. ('The exhibition space will dissolve', Portikus trumpeted at the time.) By 2005's 'The Welfare Show', of which more anon, they'd begun the large-scale, faked-up environments for which they are increasingly renowned [ill. 41–46]. Indeed, Elmgreen & Dragset's project for the Victoria and Albert Museum, 'Tomorrow' – which pulls works from the museum's collection (as well as pieces by the artists and antique-market finds) into its fictionalising orbit – sits directly in this constructed-interior lineage. Arranging furniture, rugs, embroideries, armour, ceramics, busts and much more across five rooms, it turns them into the replicated apartment of a retired architect [ill. 1–8]. 'The curators invited us, in 2009, to work within the institution', says Michael Elmgreen over coffee in London's theatre district.

> We found the former textile gallery, which for a few years had been closed for renovation, and we imagined someone living there, with the guards having a little corner. We thought about what we could turn it into, and it reminded us of grand mansion apartments in South Kensington. We thought, too, about the changes in London over recent decades, where the old upper class have somehow been squeezed out by the new money coming into the city.

The rooms became the home of the elderly, sickly Norman Swann, who was born into money, inherited his father's cache of artefacts and tried to have an independent life as a serious, socially minded architect, but failed. ('He went too far from his comfort zone', reckons Elmgreen of the artists' Proustian-named creation.) We know all this via a booklet that accompanies the show, containing a script worked up with professional playwright Leo Butler. Symbolically set just before midnight, the play is a three-hander between Norman, Daniel – his former student, a brash young interior designer and self-made man who is buying his flat from him, *objets d'art* and all – and Wendy, a waitress whom Daniel has brought to the flat. The characters, exemplifying social positions (the upper class, neo-liberalism, working-class horse sense), prickle against each other. While the dialogue is frequently funny, the humour is wine-dark and vinegar-sour.

That said, '"Tomorrow" can absolutely be viewed without reading the script', Elmgreen stresses.

> It just adds one element; if you want to make your own story from looking at the objects, you can. And if you sit on the couch and take a book from the bookshelf, another viewer can look at you and suddenly you're an actor. We've made this exhibition like a film set: we always envied film-makers such as Ingmar Bergman or Michael Haneke for their ability to describe something wider, like cultural tendencies, by showing one life, the failure in just one life. So what you can see are all the traces of a life that didn't turn out the way he, Norman, expected it. In this big apartment, the architect's study is

just a small part of it, part of the kitchen that's divided off, containing models that never turned into houses. It's a bit of a crazy man's study, filled up with dreams and desires. There are unpaid bills, old love letters, passports, travel tickets and other fabrications; there's a leak from the ceiling dripping down into a bucket. Lots of things – you can spend ten minutes in it, or three hours.

For some, the theatrics might be enough, but the duo used the V&A's artefact trove to query the idea of cultural inheritance and speculate on British society circa 2013. Says curator Louise Shannon, who worked with Elmgreen & Dragset on the project:

> The V&A has always been, and will increasingly be, a place for debate and discussions around design and contemporary life. It is crucial that we have voices such as Elmgreen & Dragset within the walls of the museum: they allow our visitors to ponder issues about cultural heritage, about objects and what it means to collect, both on a personal and national level.

According to Elmgreen, 'the personal aspect of the collection inspired us a lot. The non-scientific, non-historical element of it led us to make something in which different styles would be mixed. Fake, real, Georgian-style, the 1950s …' And this constructed coexistence of times, accompanied by a dramaturgical confrontation between old and new money, sets up 'Tomorrow' as a mirror to what Elmgreen & Dragset see as a 'very schizophrenic' moment for Britain, in which tomorrow seems hard to envision.

'There's a sentimentality in Britain, it seems, about the aura of the empire', Elmgreen says.

> All the hoopla around the Queen's Jubilee, for example, and it doesn't really reflect the reality in the streets or the country's position in world politics. So 'Tomorrow' is also about not being able to come to terms with what's happened in the world, and within Britain. But there's no defining of good and bad in the work. There's only one 'guilty' element, and that's the physical setting' [the collection Norman has inherited, symbolic of an idea of nationhood passed down, held on to] which has made everyone suffer for generations, somehow. We're not saying the old order or the new one is better, just reflecting what we, as outsiders, have noticed as a confusion of national identity here; more confused than ever, it seems. What people are proud of has nothing to do with their own lives, and vice versa.

Such judgments, of course, sit in a long tradition (from Alexis de Tocqueville's *Democracy in America* of 1835–40 through Bill Bryson and beyond) of foreigners taking stock of another nation. 'At least it's something new if you understand it in a qualified way', Elmgreen says of their perspective. (He lives part of the time in London, Dragset full-time in Berlin.) 'I'm really good at misunderstanding philosophy, for example, but then something new comes out of it. So probably our view of British culture is quite "off", but it might have something that a local viewpoint wouldn't.'

Don't think, either, that the provocation – outsiders telling locals how their country looks, not wholly adoringly – is by happenstance. If there's one thing that Elmgreen & Dragset enjoy, it's setting cats among pigeons in full public view.

In the chamber play that accompanies 'Tomorrow', Norman and Daniel come across like two articulate monsters fighting in a sack: among other things, the older man appears to have patronised and bullied the younger in the past, who, now that Norman's family fortune is gone and he has to sell up, is using new-found wealth to enact his revenge. Norman, meanwhile, hates Daniel's proud philistinism. In this embittered scenario, the only stable and sensible character is Wendy, plain-spoken fan of *Despicable Me*, who, says Elmgreen, 'doesn't have this overambitious, middle-class desire for "making it" and success, and doesn't have the guilt, laziness and confusion of the upper class'.

Such a bristling dialectic between embodied positions is characteristic of 'The Welfare Show', 'The Collectors' and 'Celebrity – The One and the Many' (2010–2011) [ill. **9–13**], the so-called trilogy of remarkable socially diagnostic Elmgreen & Dragset projects of which 'Tomorrow' is a conscious continuation. In 'The Welfare Show', exhibited in changeable formats at four venues (including London's Serpentine Gallery in 2006), Elmgreen & Dragset constructed a Kafkaesque institutional nightmare of decrepit waiting rooms, smashed stairways to 'Administration', wax babies left in cots next to ATM machines and corridors full of closed doors. If this was the welfare state as broken and impassably labyrinthine, the glitzy obverse of the social spectrum was conveyed a few years later by 'The Collectors', which also featured a broken staircase: a symbol, one might think, of the widening gap between social strata.

'The Collectors' created twin homes in two national pavilions at the Venice Biennale: one a former family home, ostensibly up for sale (by Vigilante Real Estate) and a scene of marital discord. 'I will never see you again!' [ill. 17] was scrawled on a mirror, not far from an architect's drawing board; half-burned correspondence sat in a fireplace; some furniture was draped, other pieces charred. The second 'home', meanwhile – spacious, low-slung, punctuated by elegant mid-century modern furniture – was studded with artworks and guest-starred a young nude man, a clue to the owner's tastes (alongside, say, Tom of Finland drawings), sitting reading and listening to headphones. But again all was not well: see the dead collector, 'Mr B', face-down in the pool [ill. 15].

Wealth here appears to spawn more unhappiness than it soothes. Meanwhile, and not irrelevantly, we, the viewers, are encouraged to prospect the scene voyeuristically, immersed in a prurient fantasy of the careening lifestyles of rich others. And as long as we inhabit this fantasy of wealth undercut protectively by *Schadenfreude* – the balance on which celebrity gossip magazines depend – we're not pursuing our own lives or contributing to society. That's the boomeranging nature of spectatorship, and the moral thrust, in Elmgreen & Dragset's installations: to take them in you have to engage in the kind of viewing that's being critiqued.

Nowhere in the trilogy was this more apparent than in 'Celebrity – The One and the Many', another work of two halves. One half was a fabricated four-storey apartment block, fitted within the high-ceilinged exhibiting institution. Most of this was inaccessible: one peered, through windows on the ground floor and from two mezzanine floors, into rooms that betrayed, first, their inhabitants' fascination with celebrity culture and fame (posters, TV shows, a boy sleeping under a heavy metal poster while his guitar rested on an amp) and, secondly, their atomisation and boxed-off isolation from each other.

The project's other half, meanwhile, anticipated the petrified ambience of 'Tomorrow', simulating what appeared to be an upper-class ballroom. Behind mullioned doors, inaccessible to viewers, silhouetted figures stood; we were left with maids (or, rather, golden sculptures in maids' costumes), a big bright chandelier, a live guard and a fireplace above which sat a portrait of a boy in an Eton uniform. Crouching miserably inside the fireplace was an intricate fibreglass replica of the youth himself. The poorer gaze through glass at the rich, the rich are unreachable and, amid the younger generation at least, unhappy. The golden maid and the schoolboy portrait reappear in 'Tomorrow'. (Daniel, he decides, is keeping the painting.)

'It seems like we can't stop', says Elmgreen:

> Having worked as a duo for such a long time, we have great pleasure in creating these third personas, such as Norman or the young boy in the fireplace.

This time, though, we have allowed ourselves
to be less thematic. There are a lot of different
themes. There's still this dialectical position
about the loss of old values such as the welfare
state – as in 'The Welfare Show' – but also
it's very critical of neo-liberal tendencies.
The insanity of celebrity obsession, too, will
come in a little, as in the 'Celebrity' show: this
obsession with your own individual success.

'Basically', smiles Elmgreen, 'we think people are very
bad citizens. And the idea of being part of society has
slowed down throughout the years. On Facebook, everyone promotes themselves as a superstar, and of course
people are special, but they have to realise that they're part
of a world, part of a society, and need to contribute to it.'

As Elmgreen admits, the unravelling of the economic
safety net of social security is indivisible from this need
to promote oneself, just as one can't separate dreaming
idly of wealth, or reflex nostalgia for other times, from
the precarious economic circumstances that many people now inhabit. Nor is the fact that so many individuals
float in a bubble of second-hand celebrity lifestyles un-
connected to the atomisation of society. The program-
matic virtue of Elmgreen & Dragset's work is that it ties
all of these aspects together, or rather shows how they
are always already interrelated. Crucially, it does so not
just within the pious art world but, as often as possible,
in the public arena and in relatively mainstream modes
of address.

Indeed, the art world, a realm of exclusion, VIPs, money and luxury, is in some ways only a microcosm of the larger world of the super-rich that fascinates so many outside of it (counting the yachts at the Venice Biennale, it can appear to be merely the playground of the rich). Elmgreen & Dragset have been closing doors in our faces since the early 2000s: see *Sorry We're Out of Business* (2002), a mock-up of a closed gallery shopfront; *Closing Time* (2003), a fake shuttered bar; *Prada Marfa* (2005); and *Too Late* (2008) **[ill. 20–22]**, London's Victoria Miro Gallery made over into a convincing simulation of a gay nightclub after closing time, accoutred with locked private rooms. (The club, notably, was called 'The Mirror'.) Accordingly, as their work has moved outside the white cube, the themes have persisted. The cultural fascination with wealth – and specifically old wealth – that scooped such huge viewing figures for *Downton Abbey*, for example, will inevitably underwrite some of the hands-on attention that 'Tomorrow' receives, even as the work puts such attention into question.

For Elmgreen, a TV programme such as *Downton* reflects what they, as artists, are up against, both outside the art world and within it. 'I read a *Guardian* article a couple of years ago entitled "The New Boredom"', he says, 'about a fear of being genuinely eccentric, (*'Downton Abbey* not only depicts a reactionary social order; it helps to create one', Stuart Jeffries wrote.) 'It's a no-go, the writer said, and that was why this very sentimental, harmless series was so popular, with its old values about being scaled-down, not sticking out too much. And it goes on in the art world as well; today, you're not allowed to be loud, or eccentric.

I loved that article, and when we started to work on this show – well, it's there.' Hence the highly undomesticated domesticity (and formal unusualness) of 'Tomorrow', which has less in common with Julian Fellowes than with Vivian Stanshall's uproarious upper-class satire *Sir Henry at Rawlinson End* (1978), or the thoroughgoing critiques of national psyches in, say, Thomas Bernhard's novels or the Haneke films that Elmgreen & Dragset cite as inspiration.

'Their work,' says Shannon, 'explores space, boundaries and ambiguity, which we have in tonnes at the museum. We have hierarchies of knowledge, expected etiquettes, and Elmgreen & Dragset turn these on their heads.' If one asks who, within the work's moral universe, is culpable here – well, it's complicated, and subjective. If the 'guilty' element, as Elmgreen suggests, is the setting, then the objects themselves can't be held responsible and the collectors and donors accumulated and gifted for varying reasons. These are the push-pull forces in play, 'Tomorrow' infers, and as you move through its myriad traces of privilege, class and generational guard-change, you'd be minded to examine closely your own reactions and predilections. It's nearly midnight. Norman is choking in his armchair, Daniel is contentedly ordering pepperoni pizza and Coke from Domino's, and Wendy is asking if someone should call a doctor. Where, dear viewer, do you stand?

This text was first published in *V&A Magazine*, Autumn/Winter 2013, pp.46-57.

Period Piece
(After – Tomorrow. Before – Biography)

QUINN LATIMER

His walls flee his red touch. Library lost its green.

Torch. He thinks about his things too much, he thinks.

After dinner, he prepares his remarks. The blue lecture.

Is in three years or it is never but this does not matter.

He thinks – better to be prepared. He closes the glass.

Case. Walks his suitable carpets. (They are beautiful perhaps.

Apposite for different kinds of apartments but who is.

To say, really?) Exhibition of history. His unattended.

Autobiography. He watches himself after dinner engaging.

In thoughts befitting. His profession – he forgets. Sometimes.

What it is. He. Does. And this is not helpful. Antique architectural he.

Shakes his head grimly, then affectionately. He is too hard.

On himself, he rejoins him. Self. We all are did he – aloud?

Yes. Yellow chorus: wealth of. Description. He admires such. Quirks on.

Occasion. So should one describe it: Glass case. Lucid carpets.

Of Afghanistan, some Scandinavian. The lean marble or *Zaftig*.

Figures, bowl-like. Not quite Grecian. More Eastern. Fertility.

Statuary that. Makes him blink, blanche, but they are his.

Inheritance. How. To make them. Disappear, he thinks, fingering their cold.

Clean lines. Pale surfaces. White orifices. A kind of carpet.

Cleaner, he imagines. No one here to. Offer his joke to: His fever.

What is his fever. For recollection, he summers. Fingerprints.

Flee his glass. Case. Vitrine of my feelings, he thinks. Writes it.

Down in. His leather. Notebook the one offered as a present. Two.

Summers ago. Or did he order it for himself. No tenants (except of.

The soul, he thinks.) No renters but owners. He describes his.

Gardens to himself. Work or leisure. Bridles of pleasure. That old.

Style. Its stink. He'll miss it. Next season. Walls flee yellow touch. Crockery.

Cracks. I am an old vessel. He thinks. I hate. My antique. Season.

My Review. No owners but. Renters. Fondly. Rent them fondly.

Forgivingly forgive. Yourself he. Admonishes his appointments.

Pale inheritance. Wealth of. Mannerisms – past. Manner me someone.

Should. Instruct. My modernist. Piles. Build us: they instruct. Don't mind.

Me he minds. He thanks an. Editorial board before. Dinner service.

After his red wall his antique. Tenants his vessel his. Appointments.

My period is every period. He rushes. Past. To write down in his.

Leather. Bought on a tour of. Kenya. His lecture fills. A vitrine. Lovely.
Execution. He imagines his. Audience. That gelder. *Geld*. Burnished.
Critics. So sober their. Appreciation. No tenants except of. The soul.
Studied force of. His argument, its elegance. Birds circling: films of.
Their mouths. Working. Like acid. Dark cinema of. Their work. Some.
Hover. Waiting. A kind of. Criticism. Cinema of. Sleep. He sleeps.

[ill. 1-9]

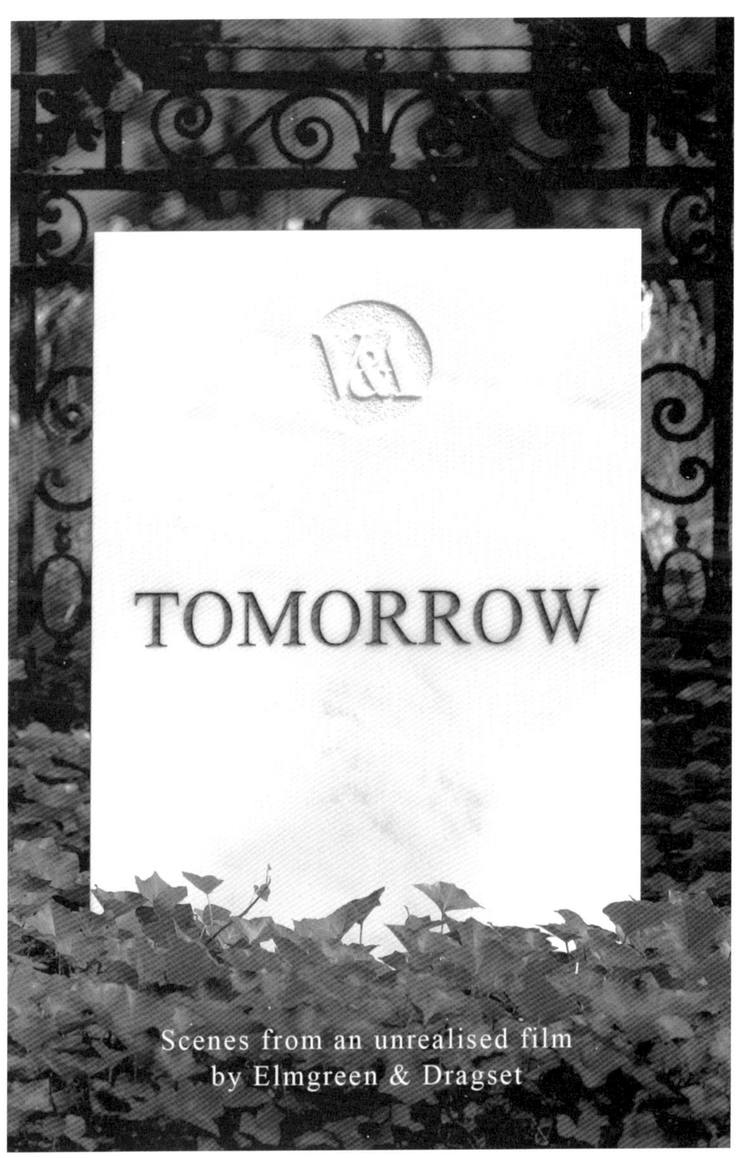

ill. 1
'Tomorrow' (script booklet cover),
Victoria and Albert Museum, London, 2013

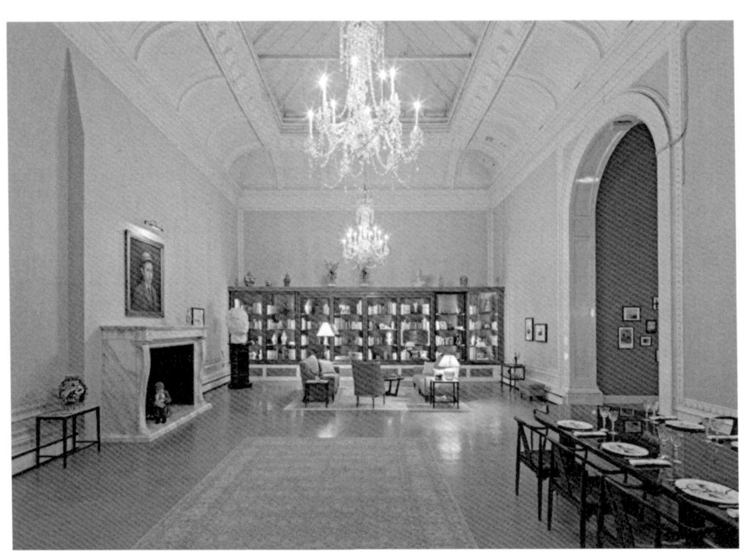

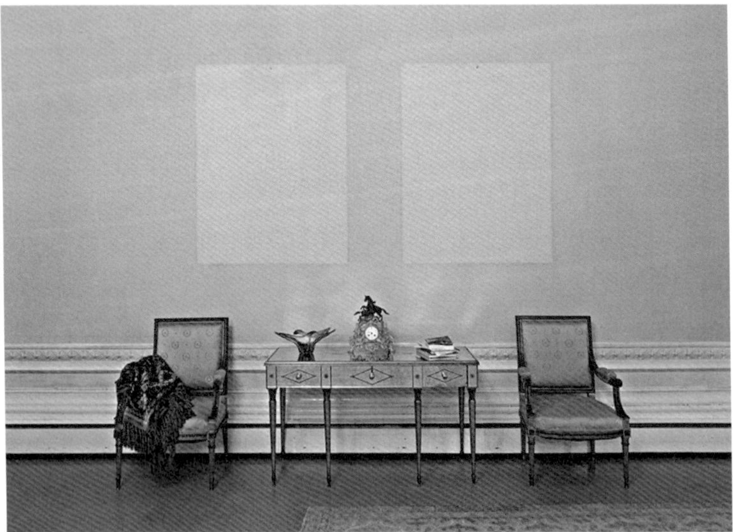

'Tomorrow' (living room),
Victoria and Albert Museum, London, 2013

ill. 3
'Tomorrow' (detail),
Victoria and Albert Museum, London, 2013

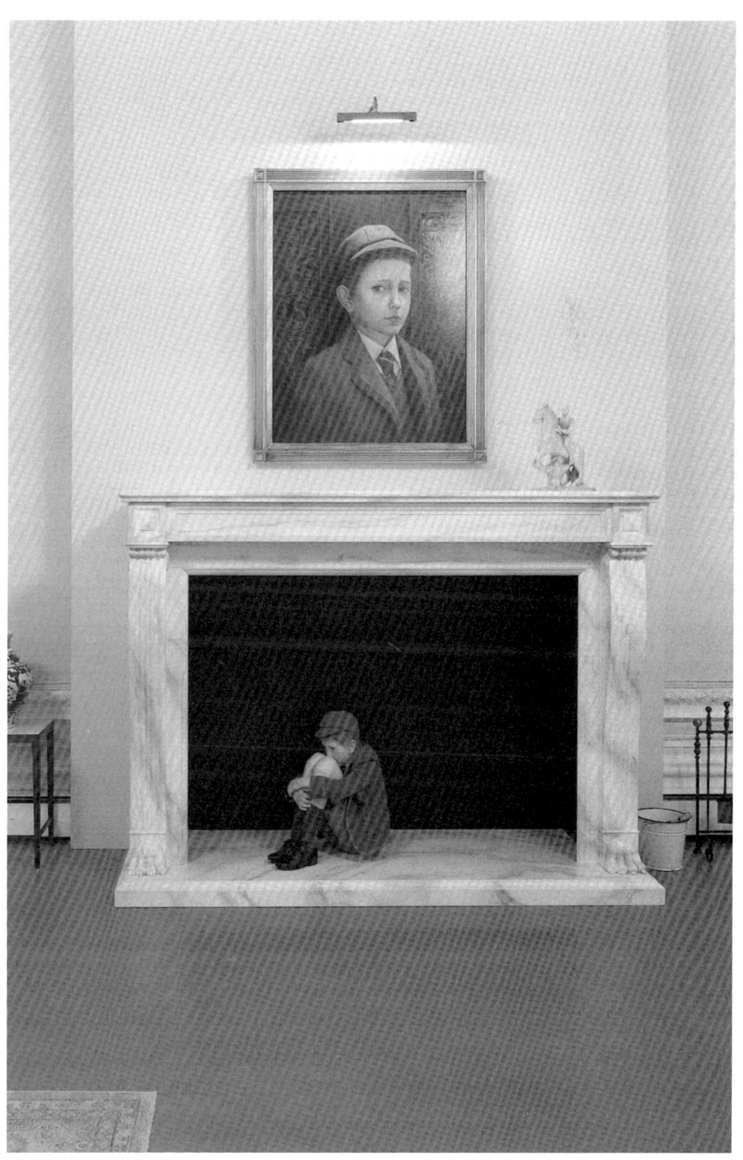

ill. 4
High Expectations, 2010

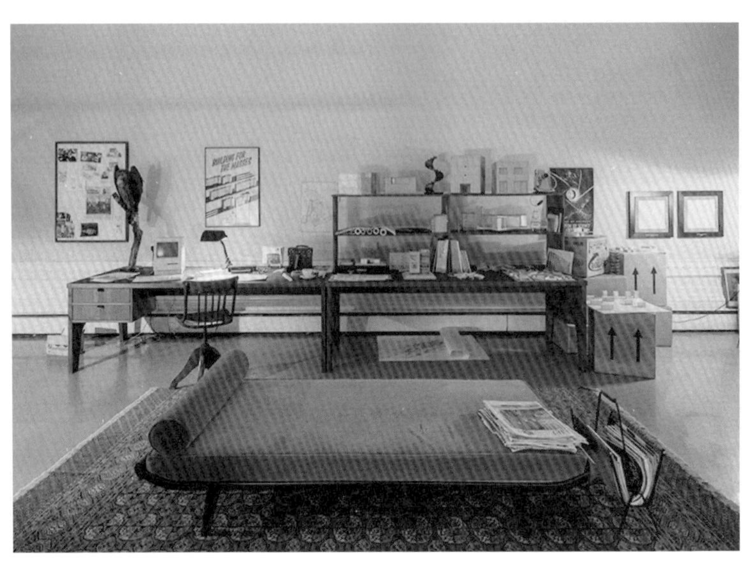

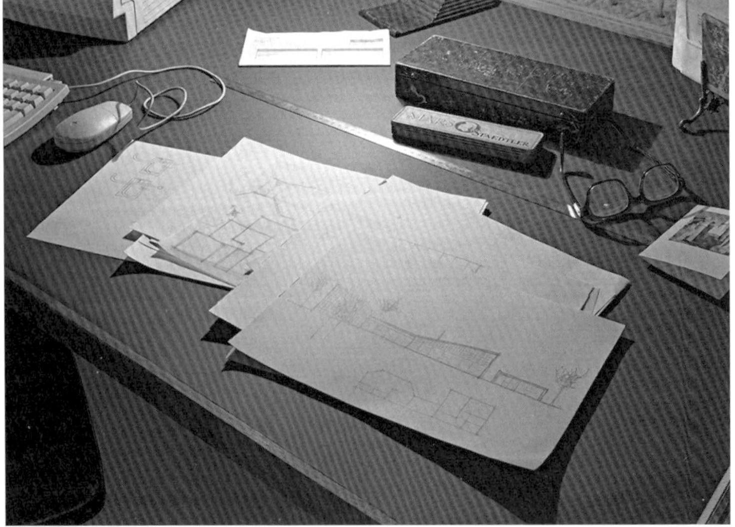

ill. 5
'Tomorrow' (studio),
Victoria and Albert Museum, London, 2013

ill. 6
'Tomorrow' (studio, detail),
Victoria and Albert Museum, London, 2013

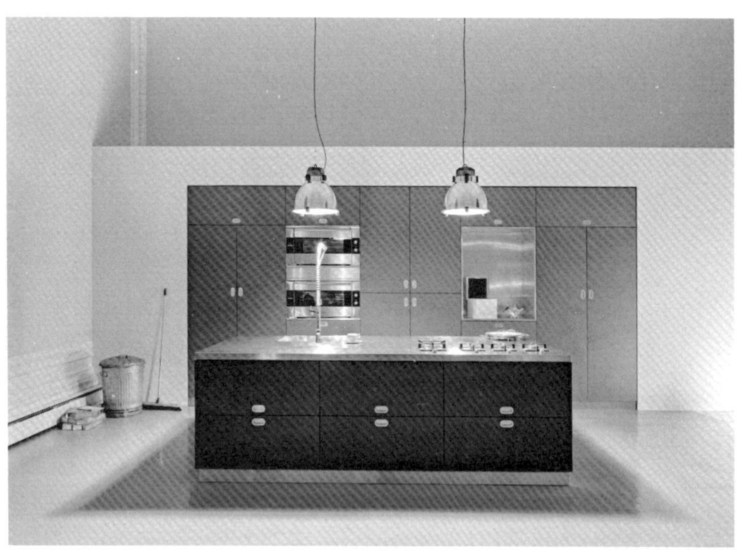

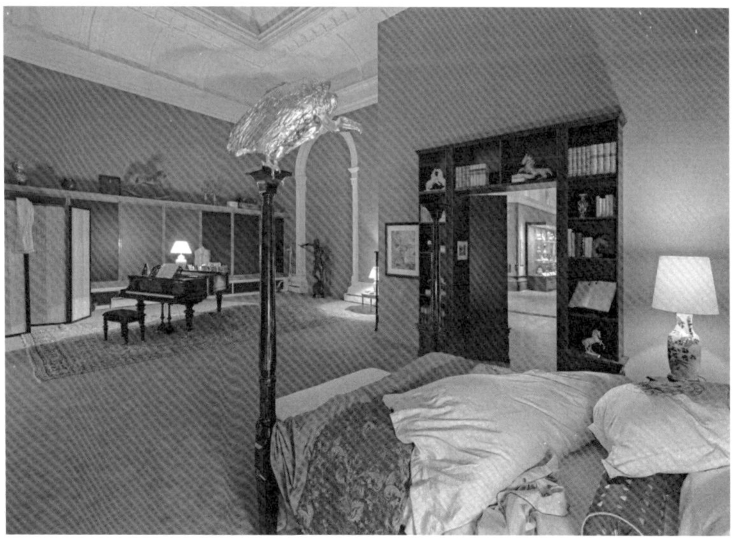

ill. 7
'Tomorrow' (kitchen),
Victoria and Albert Museum, London, 2013

ill. 8
'Tomorrow' (bedroom),
Victoria and Albert Museum, London, 2013

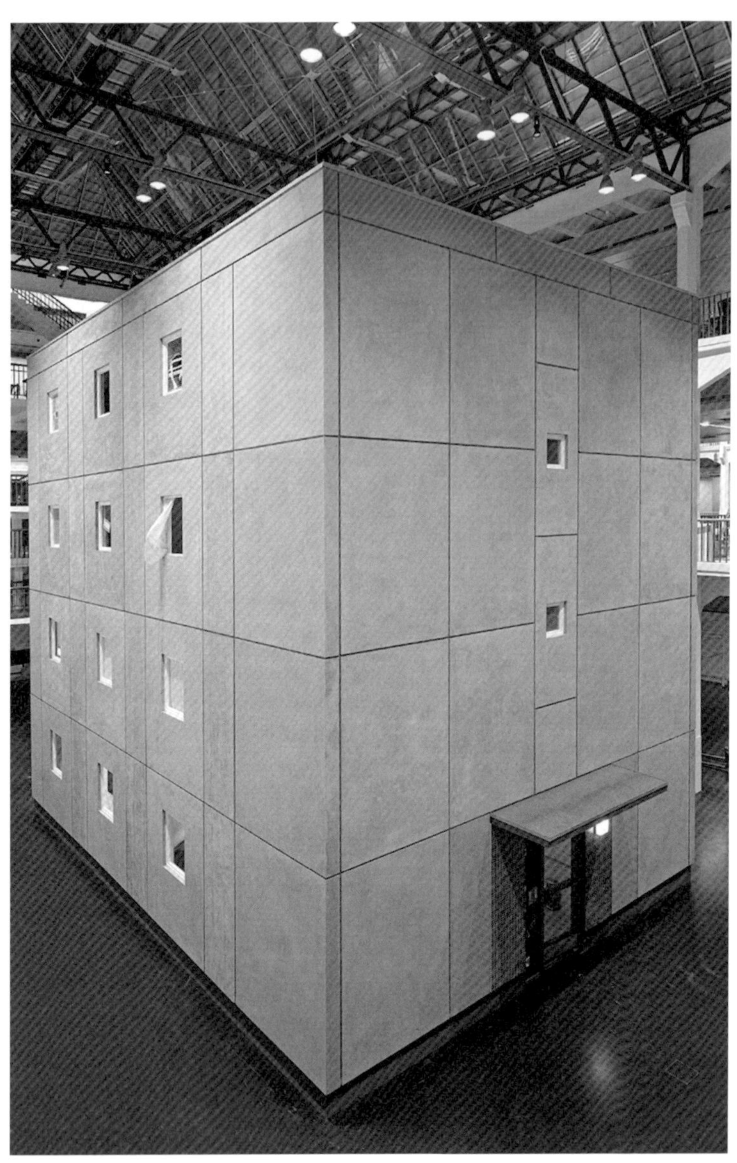

ill. 9
'Celebrity – The One & The Many',
ZKM | Museum of Contemporary Art, Karlsruhe, 2010-11

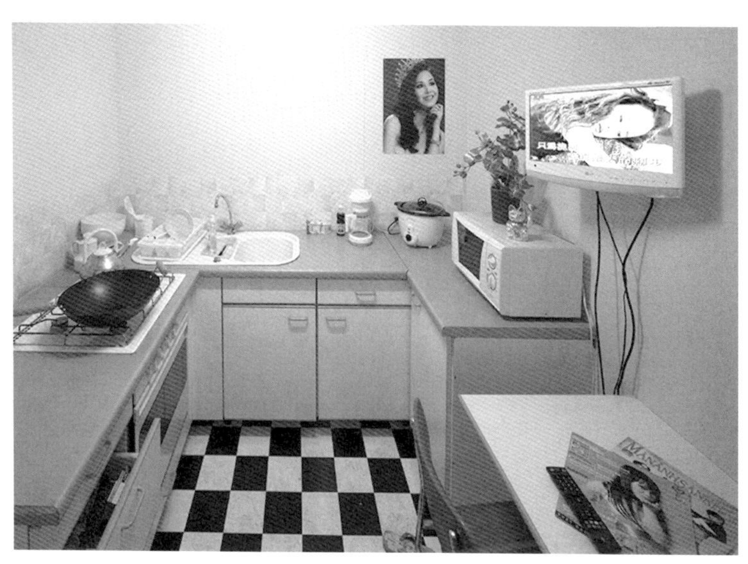

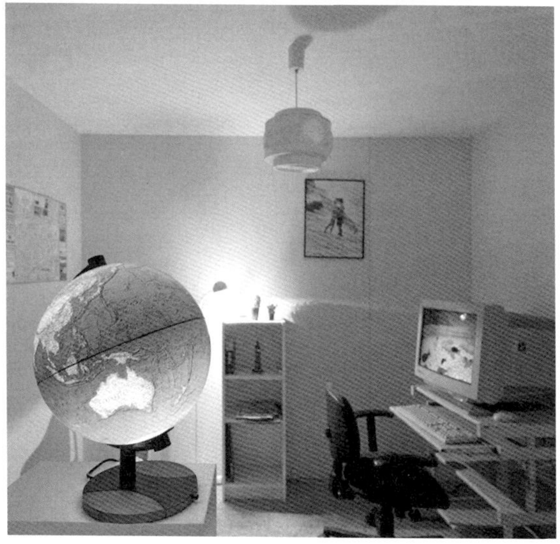

ill. 10
'Celebrity – The One & The Many' (interiors),
ZKM | Museum of Contemporary Art, Karlsruhe, 2010-11

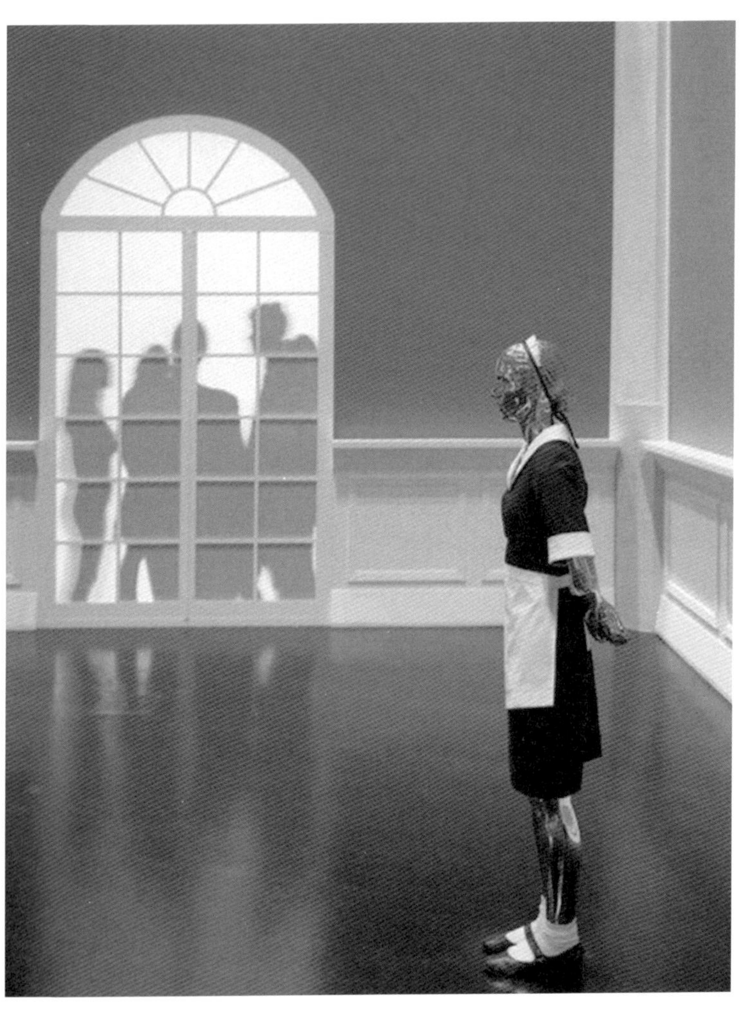

ill. 11
Irina, 2007, 'Celebrity – The One & The Many',
ZKM | Museum of Contemporary Art, Karlsruhe, 2010-11

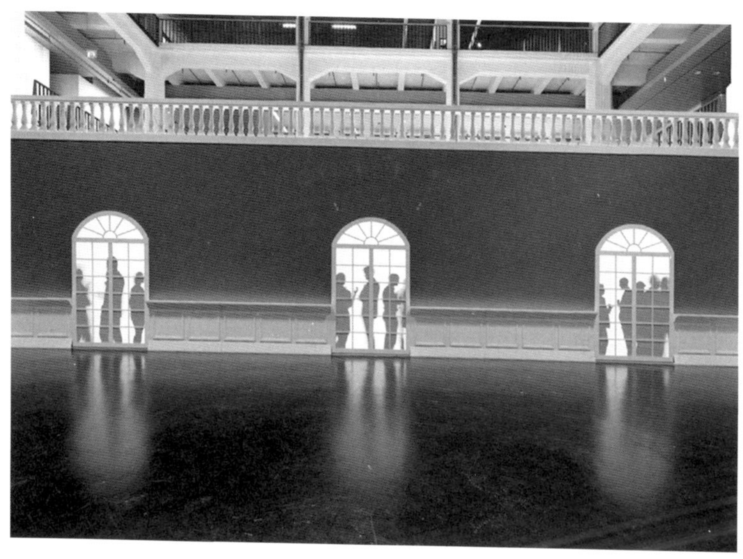

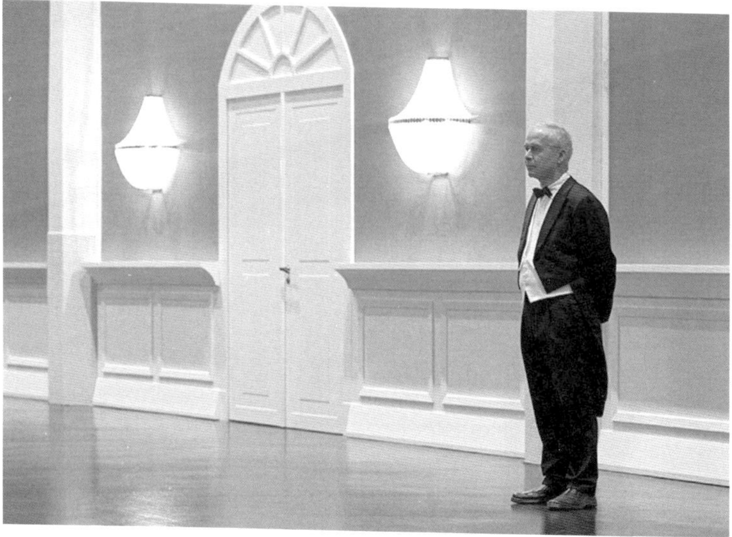

ill. 12
Reception, 2010, 'Celebrity – The One & The Many',
ZKM | Museum of Contemporary Art, Karlsruhe, 2010-11

ill. 13
Butler, 2010, 'Celebrity – The One & The Many',
ZKM | Museum of Contemporary Art, Karlsruhe, 2010-11

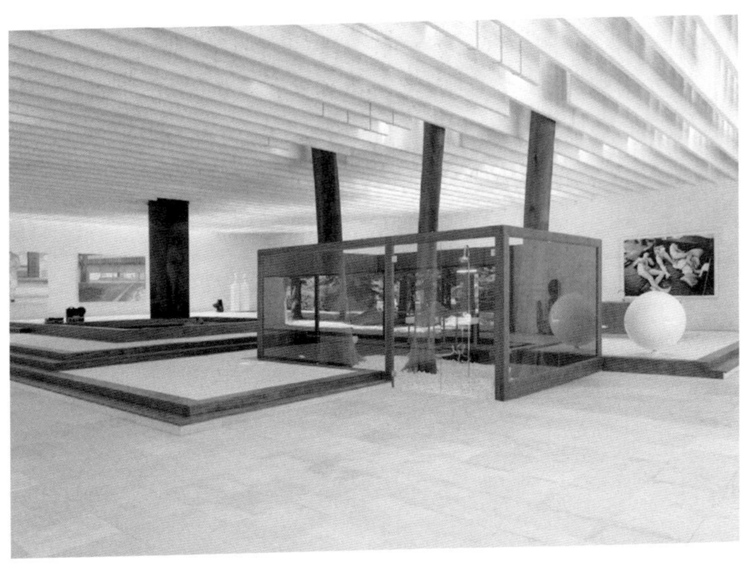

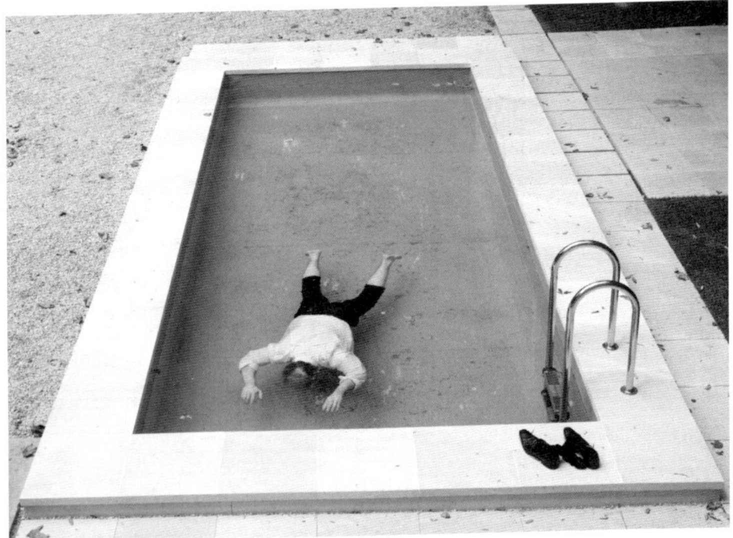

Nordic Pavilion, 'The Collectors',
53rd Venice Biennale, 2009

Death of a Collector, 2009

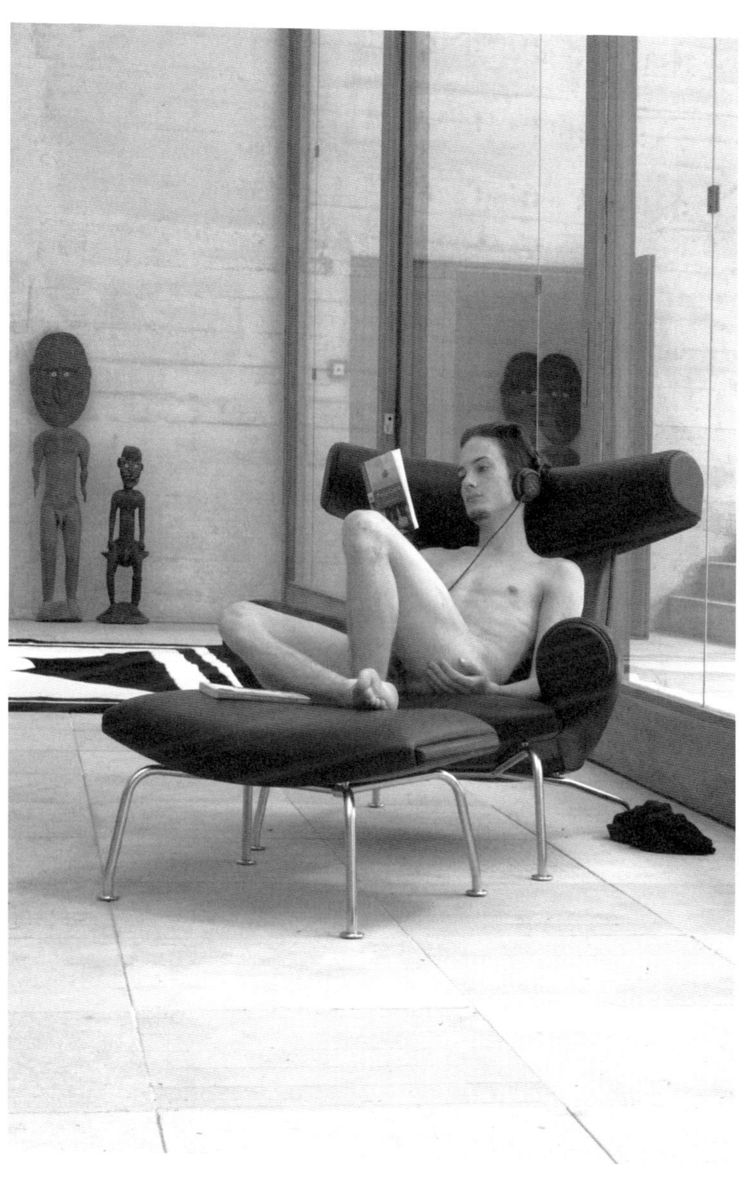

Nordic Pavilion, 'The Collectors' (detail),
53rd Venice Biennale, 2009

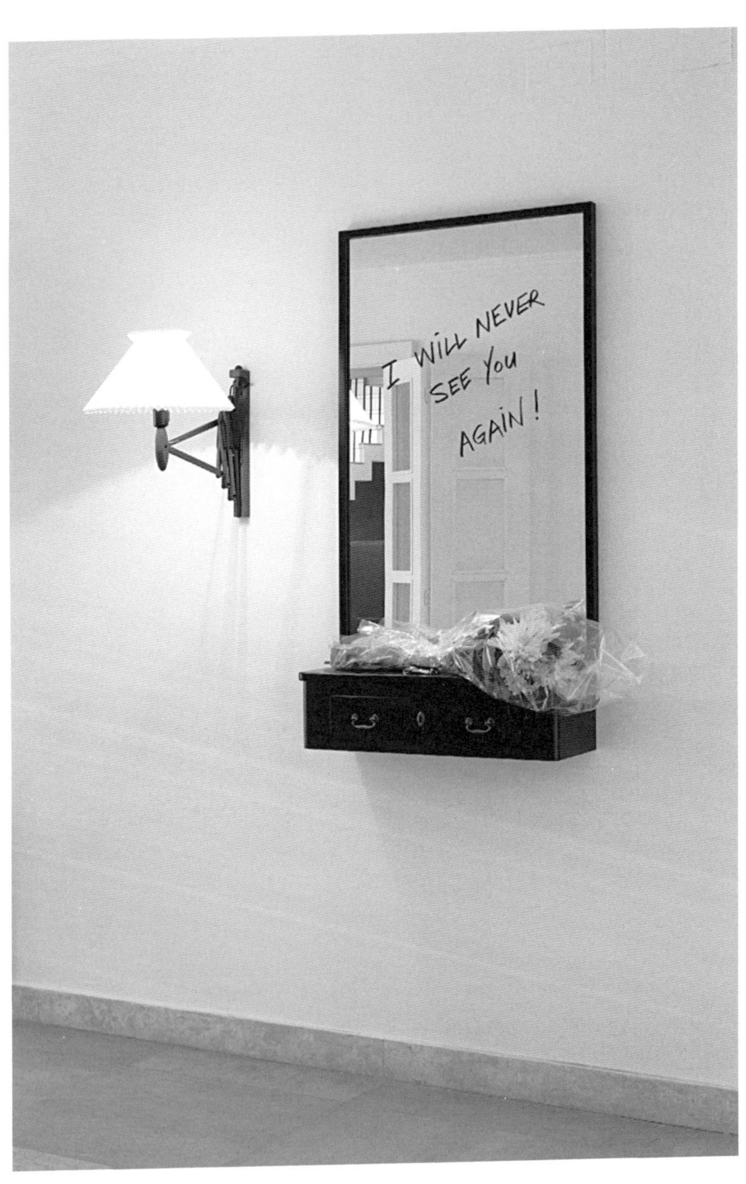

ill. 17
I will never see you again, 2009

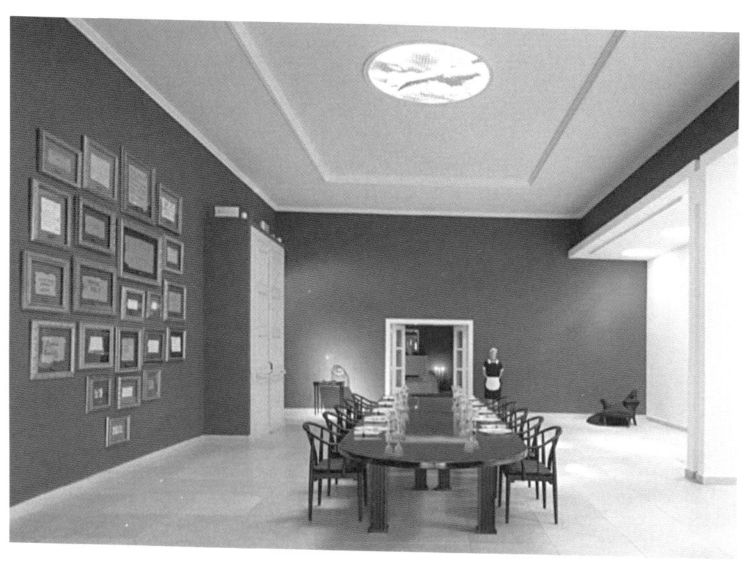

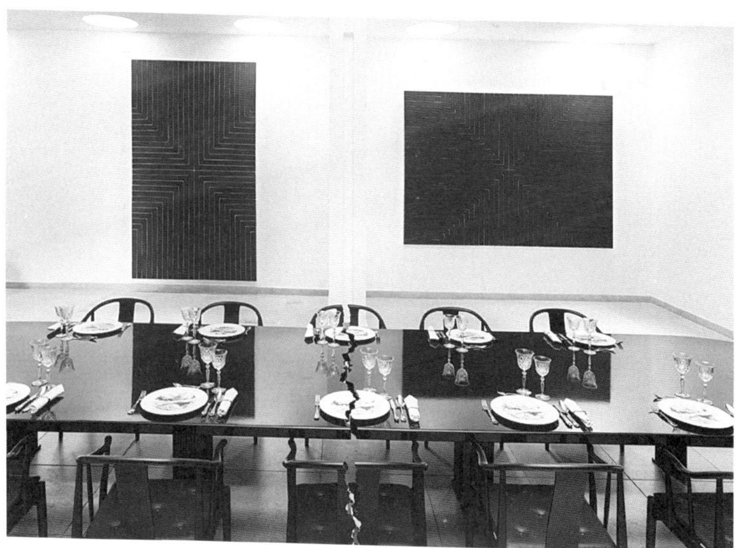

Danish Pavilion, 'The Collectors',
53rd Venice Biennale, 2009

Table for Bergman, 2009

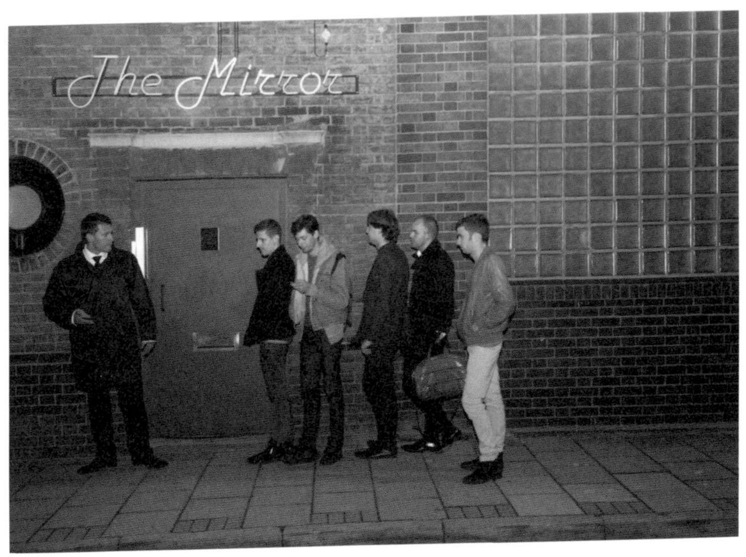

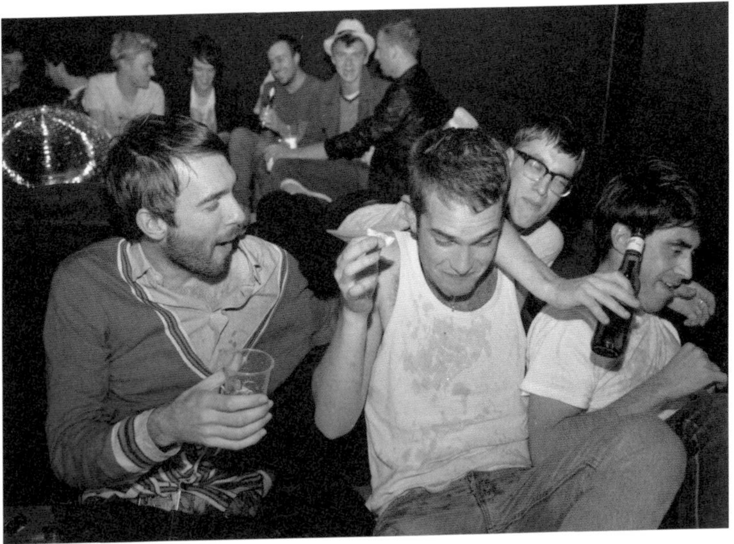

ill. 20
'Too Late', Victoria Miro Gallery,
London, 2008

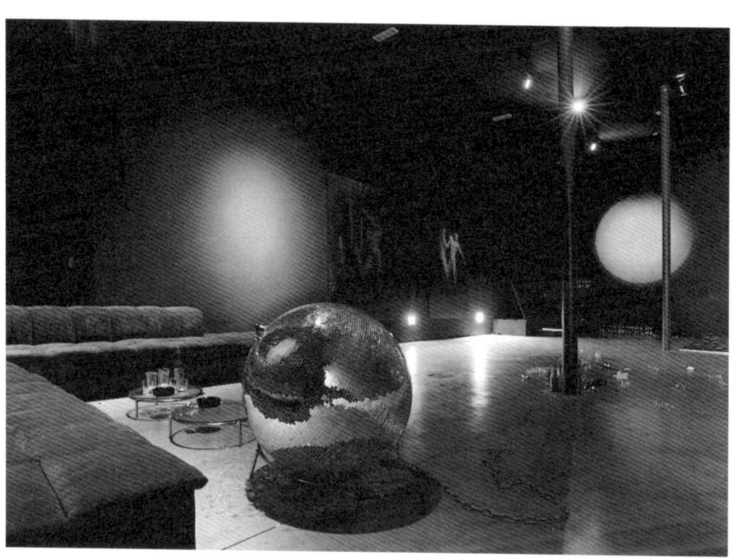

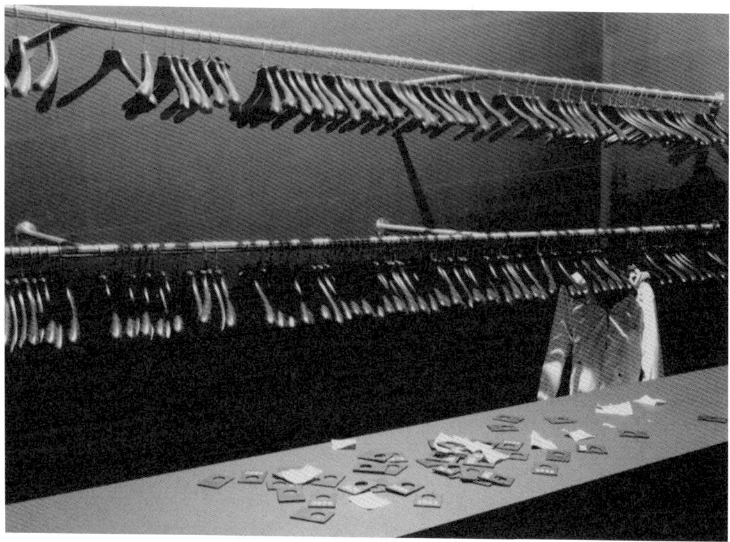

ill. 21
(Un)Lucky Strike, 2008
'Too Late', Victoria Miro Gallery, London

ill. 22
Last Guest, Fig. 3, 2008
'Too Late', Victoria Miro Gallery, London

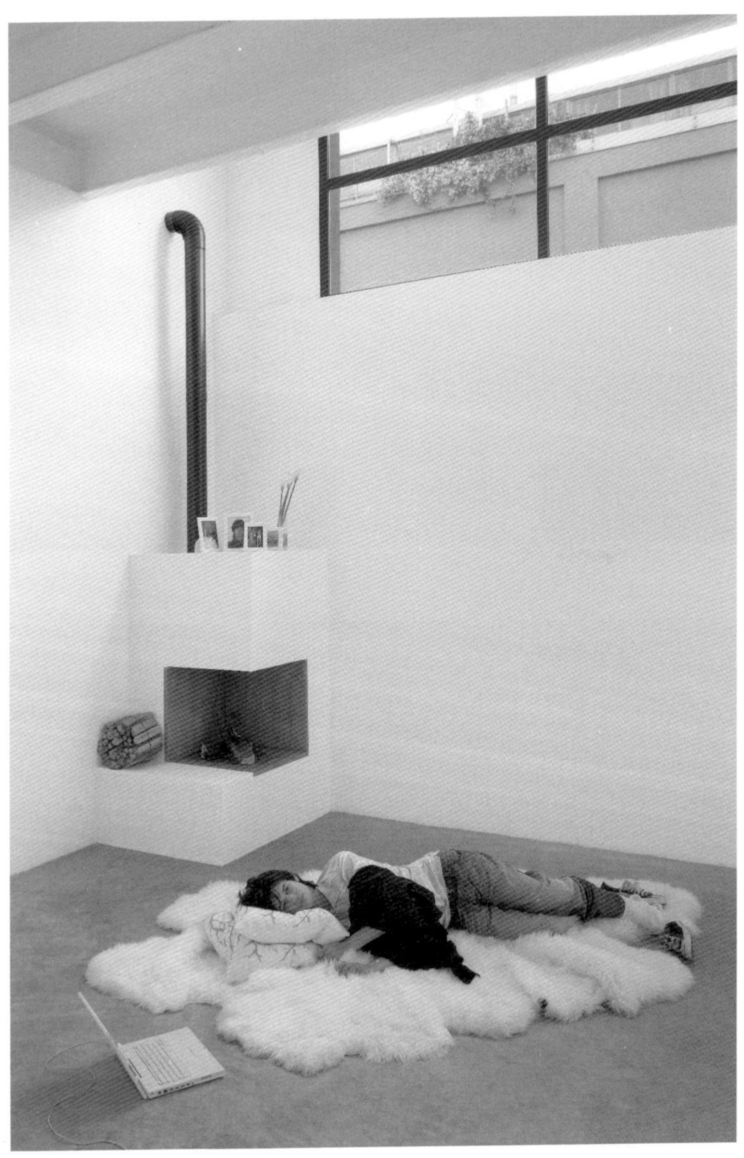

ill. 23
Andrea Candela, Fig. 1, 2006

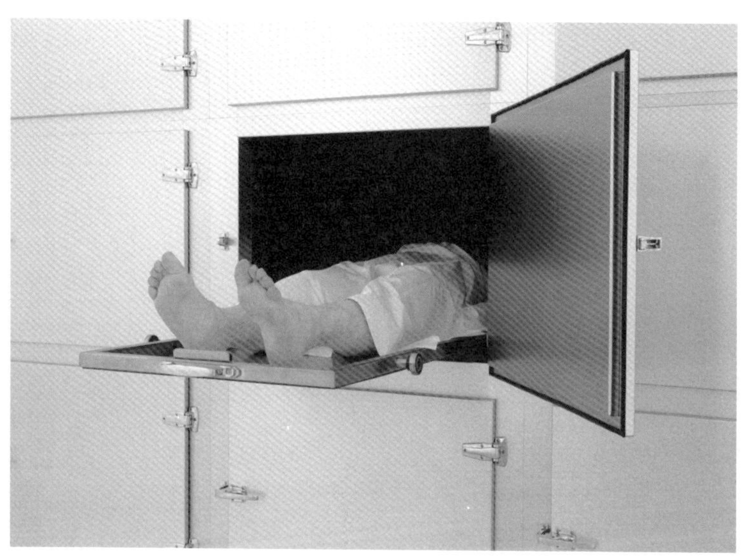

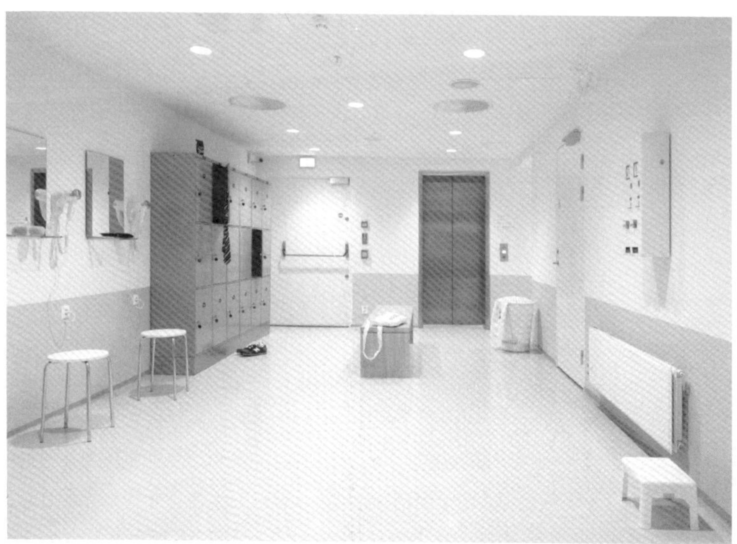

ill. 24
Untitled (The Mysterious Afterlife of Mr B), 2011

ill. 25
Amigos, 2011

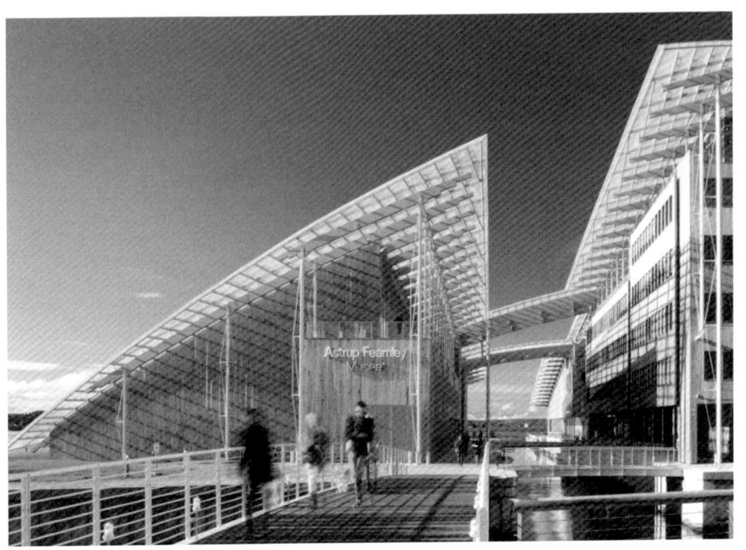

ill. 26
Astrup Fearnley Museet, Oslo

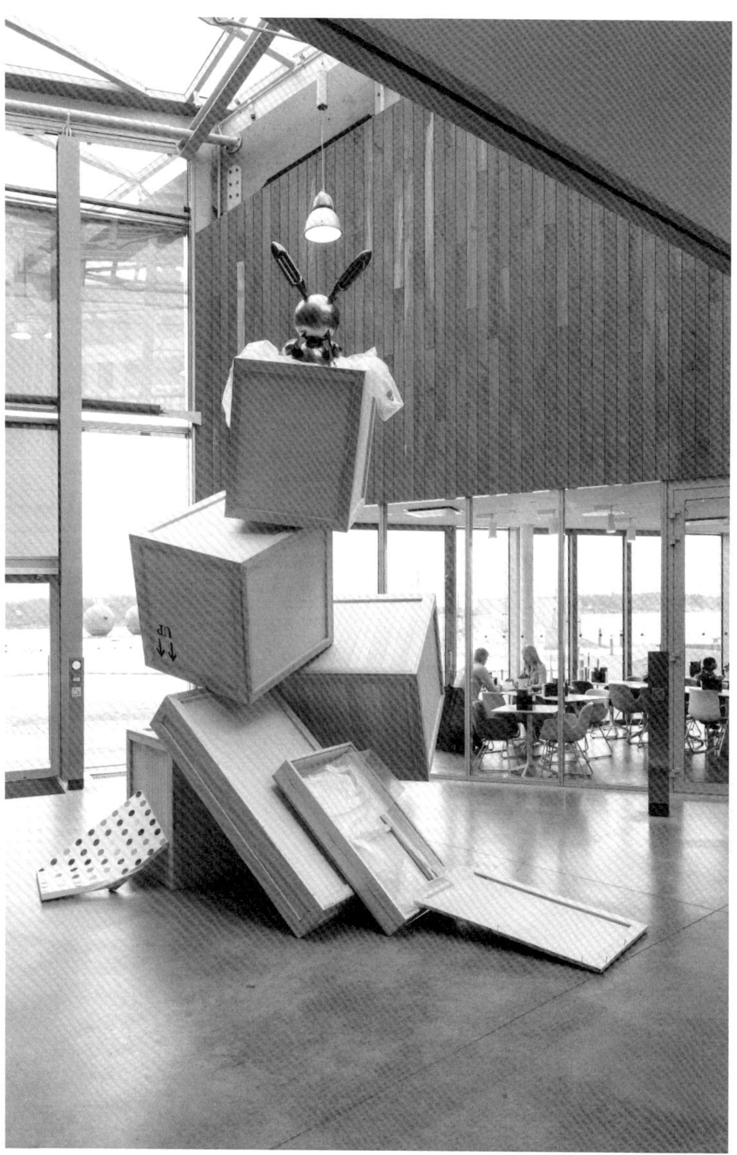

ill. 27
Crash…Boom…Bang!, 2008

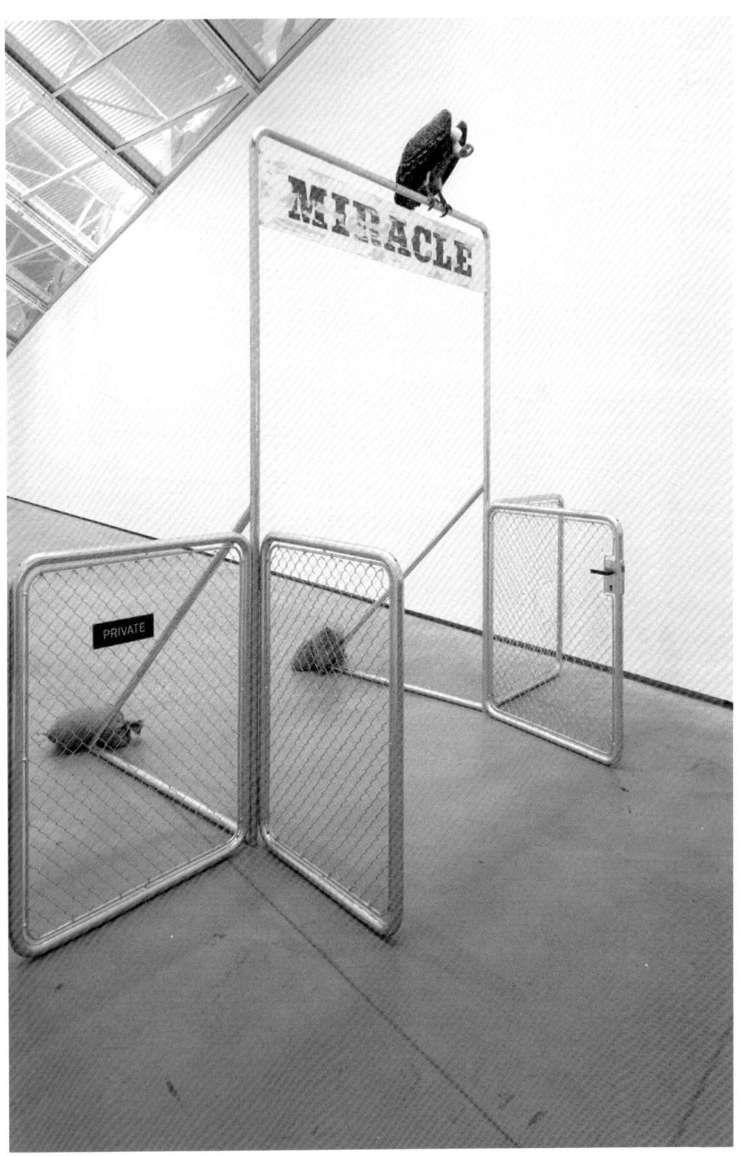

ill. 28
Rite of Passage, 2014

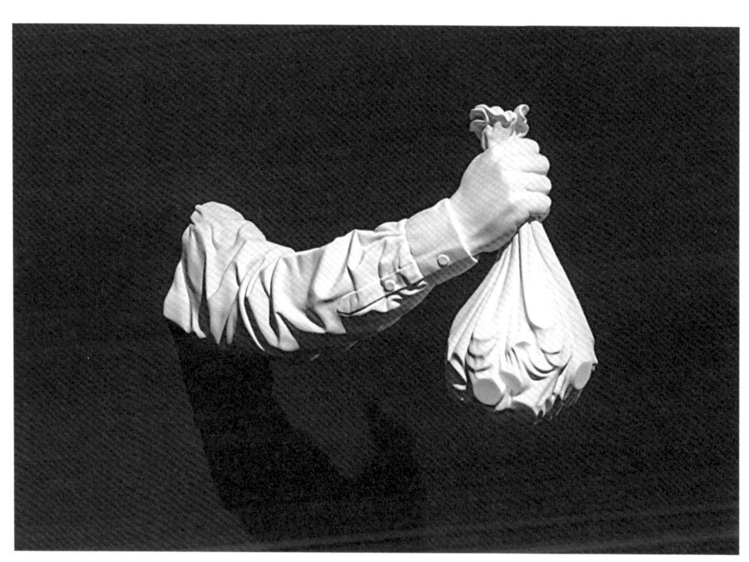

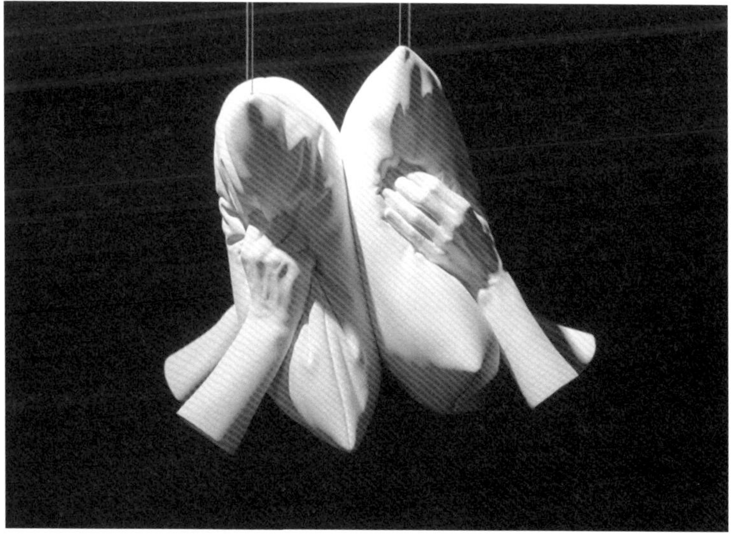

ill. **29**
Temptation, 2012

ill. **30**
The Agony and the Ecstasy, 2010

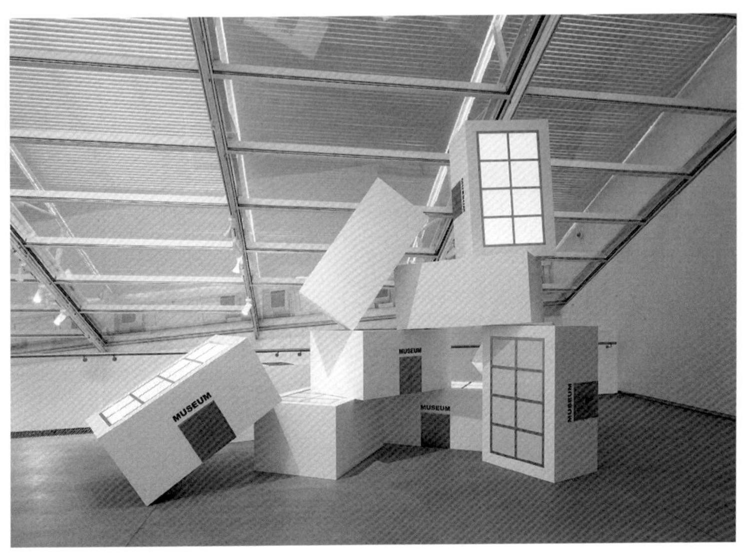

ill. 31
Powerless Structures, Fig. 529, 2014

ill. 32
The Named Series, 2012
Irina, 2007 (foreground)

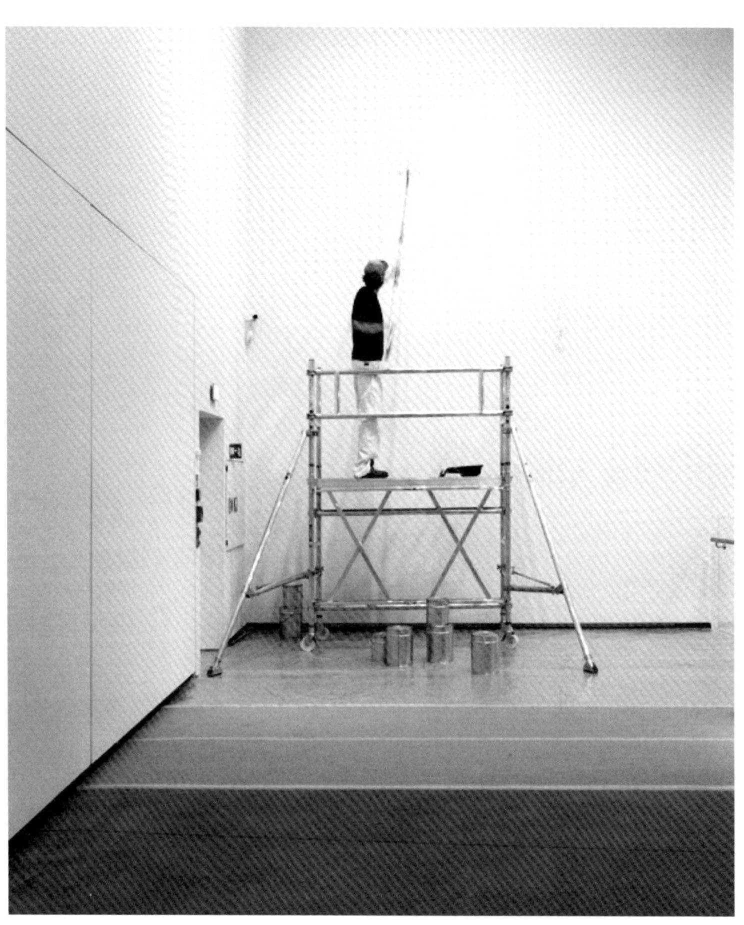

ill. 33
Zwischen anderen Ereignissen
(Between Other Events, 2000, 2014)

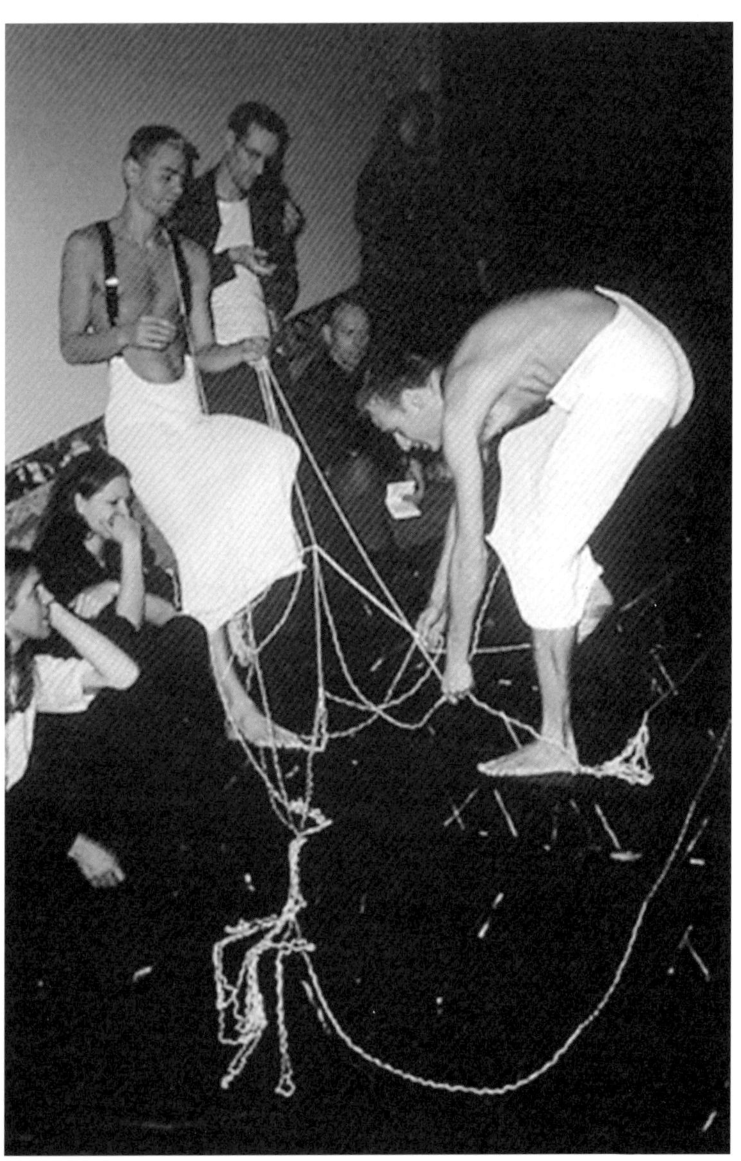

ill. 34
Untitled, 1996

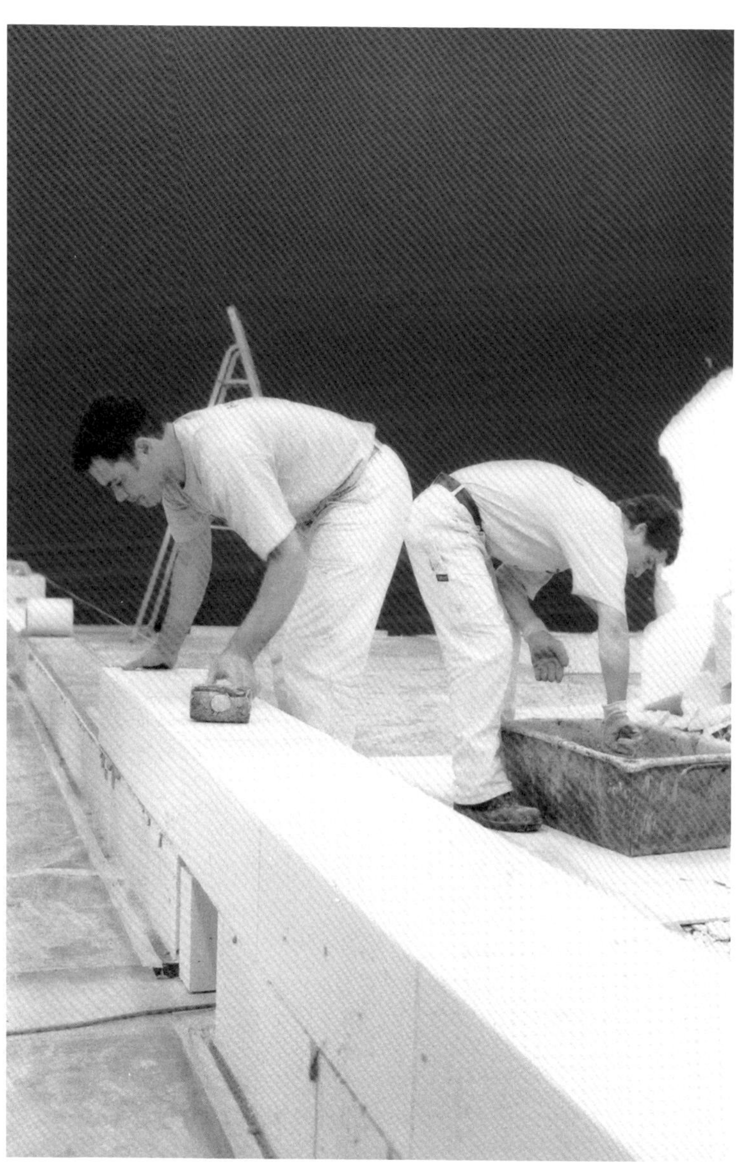

ill. 35
'Taking Place',
Kunsthalle Zürich, 2001-02

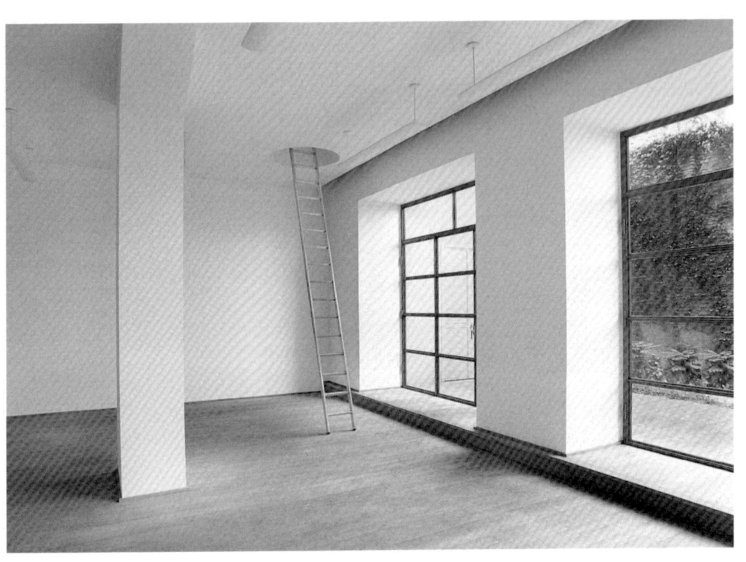

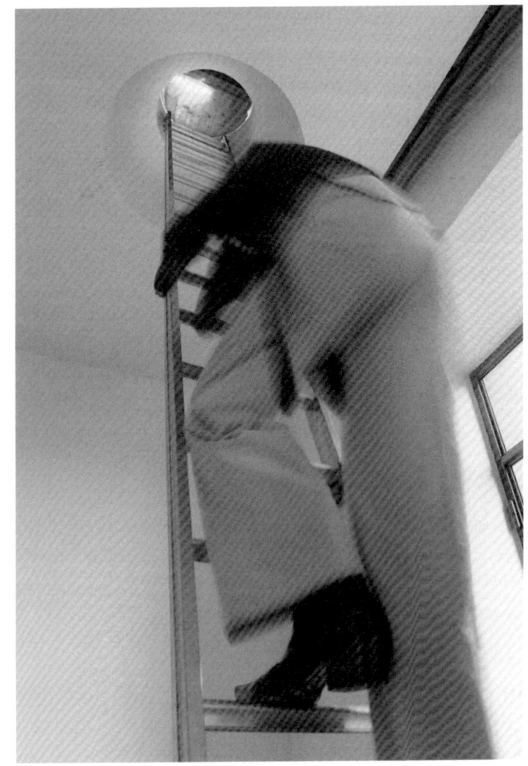

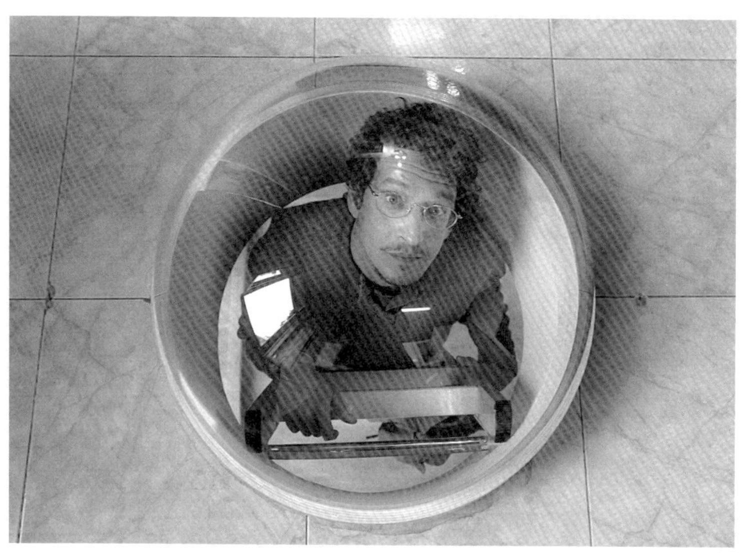

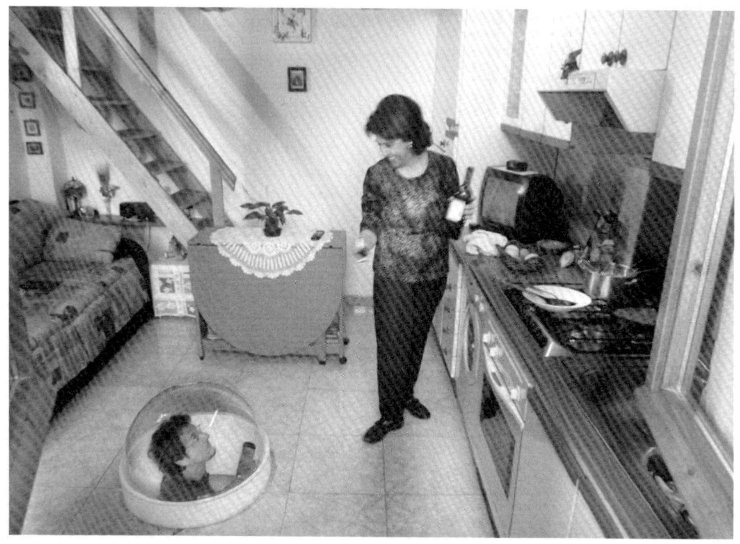

'How Are You Today?',
Galleria Massimo De Carlo, Milan, 2002

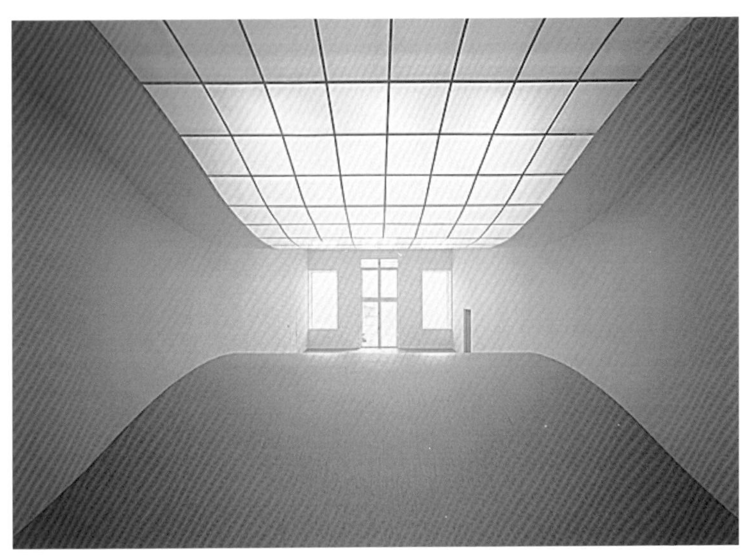

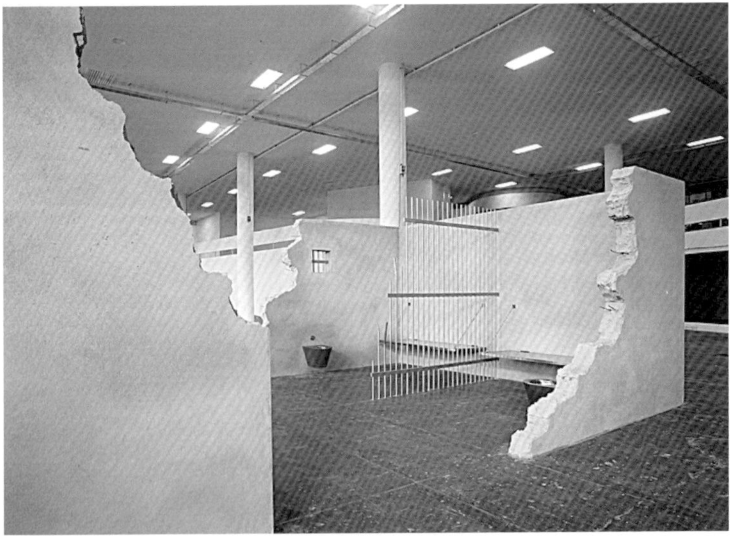

ill. 37
'Powerless Structures, Fig. 111',
Portikus, Frankfurt/Main, 2001

ill. 38
Prison Breaking/Powerless Structures, Fig. 333, 2002

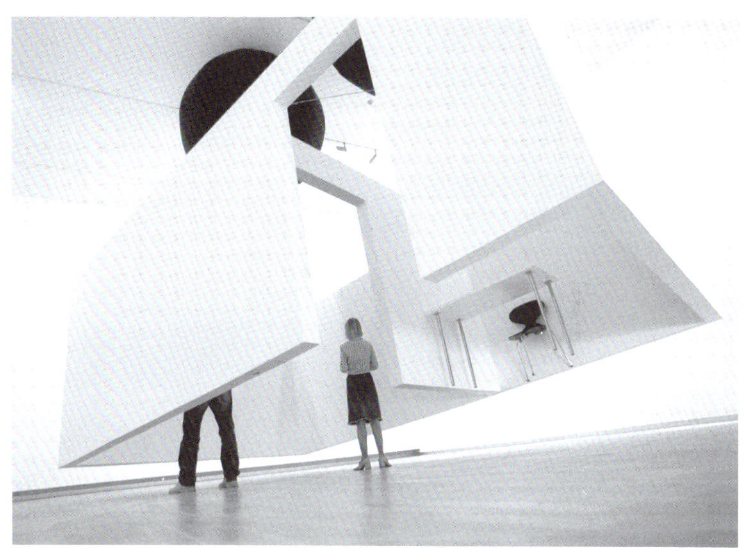

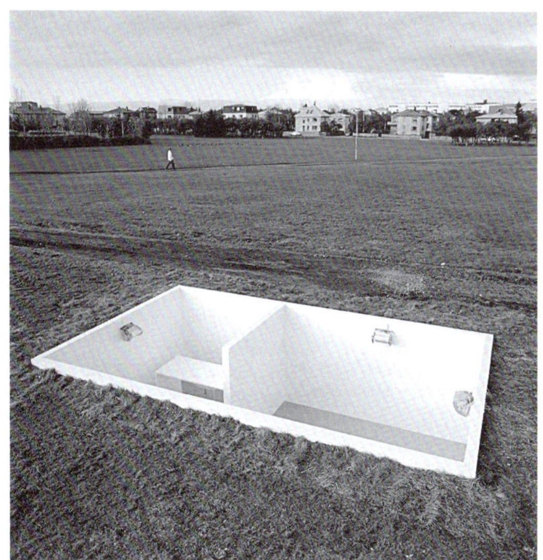

ill. 39
Elevated Gallery/Powerless Structures, Fig. 146, 2001

ill. 40
Dug Down Gallery/Powerless Structures, Fig. 45, 1998

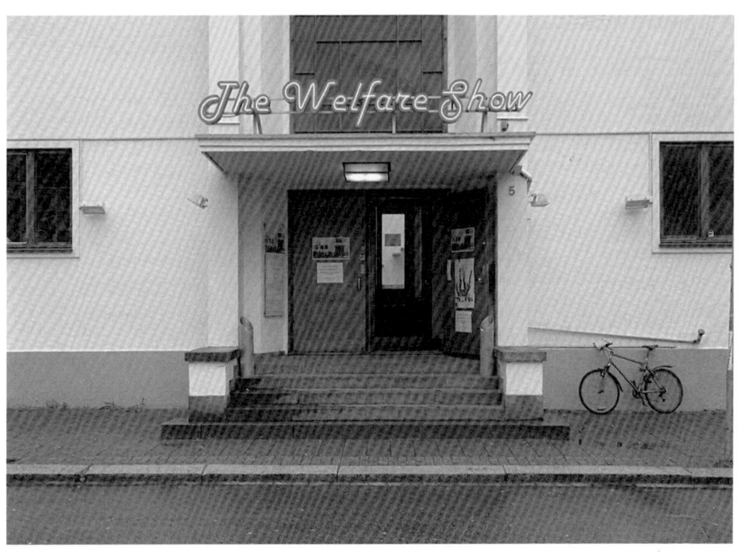

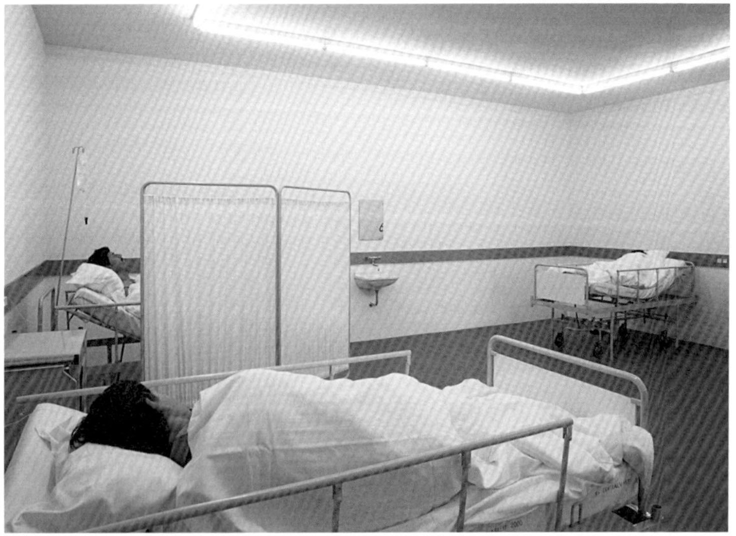

ill. 41
'The Welfare Show',
Bergen Kunsthall, 2005

ill. 42
Please, keep quiet!, 2003

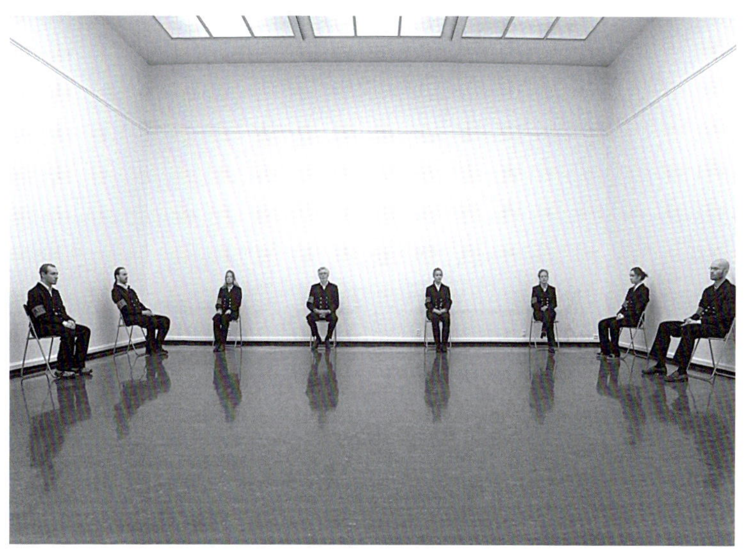

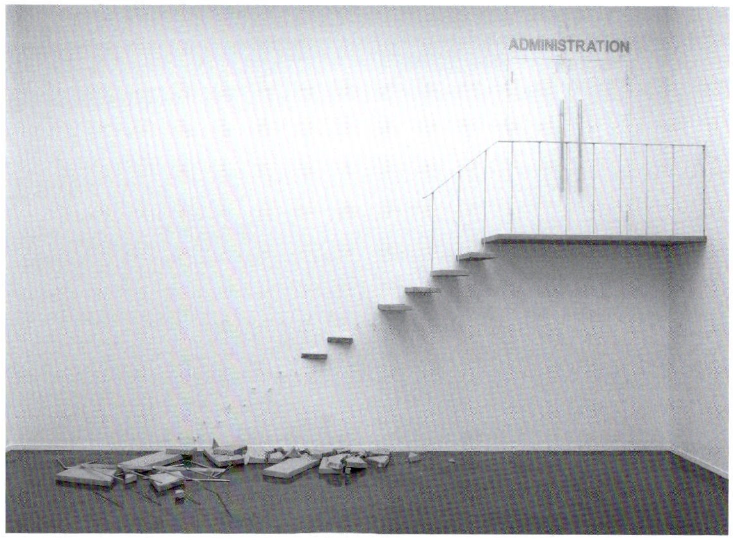

ill. 43
Re-g(u)arding the Guards, 2005

ill. 44
Social Mobility, Fig. 1, 2005

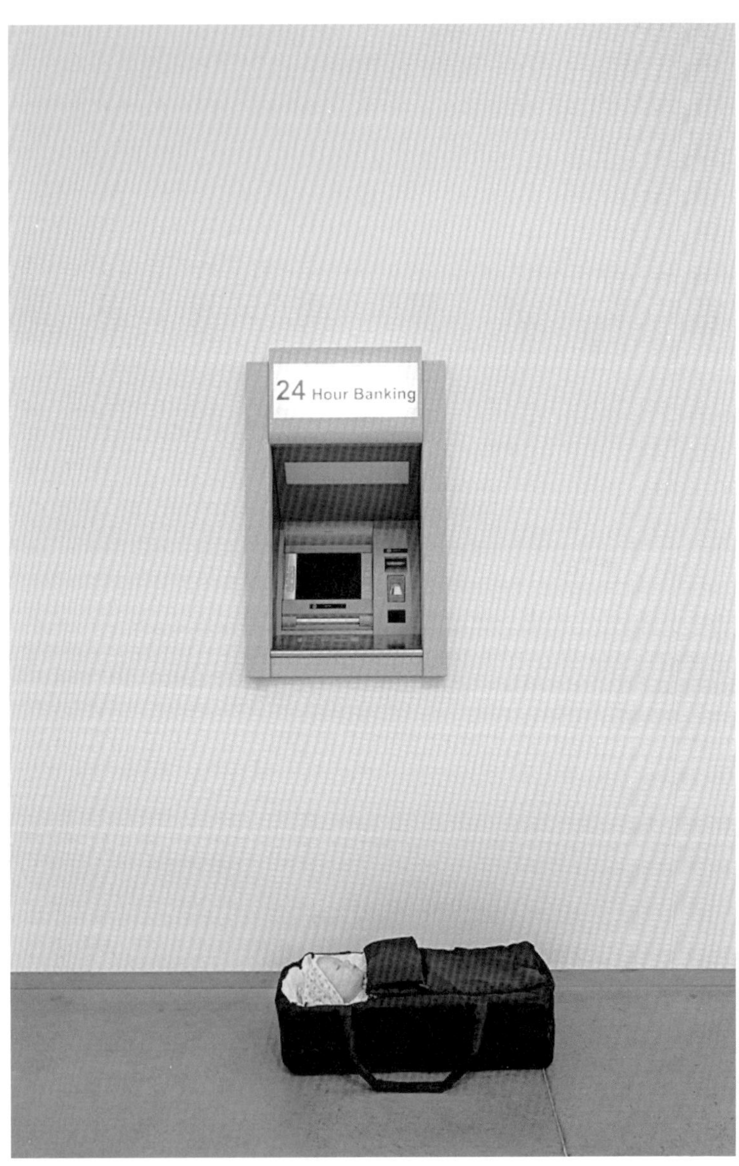

ill. 45
Modern Moses, 2006

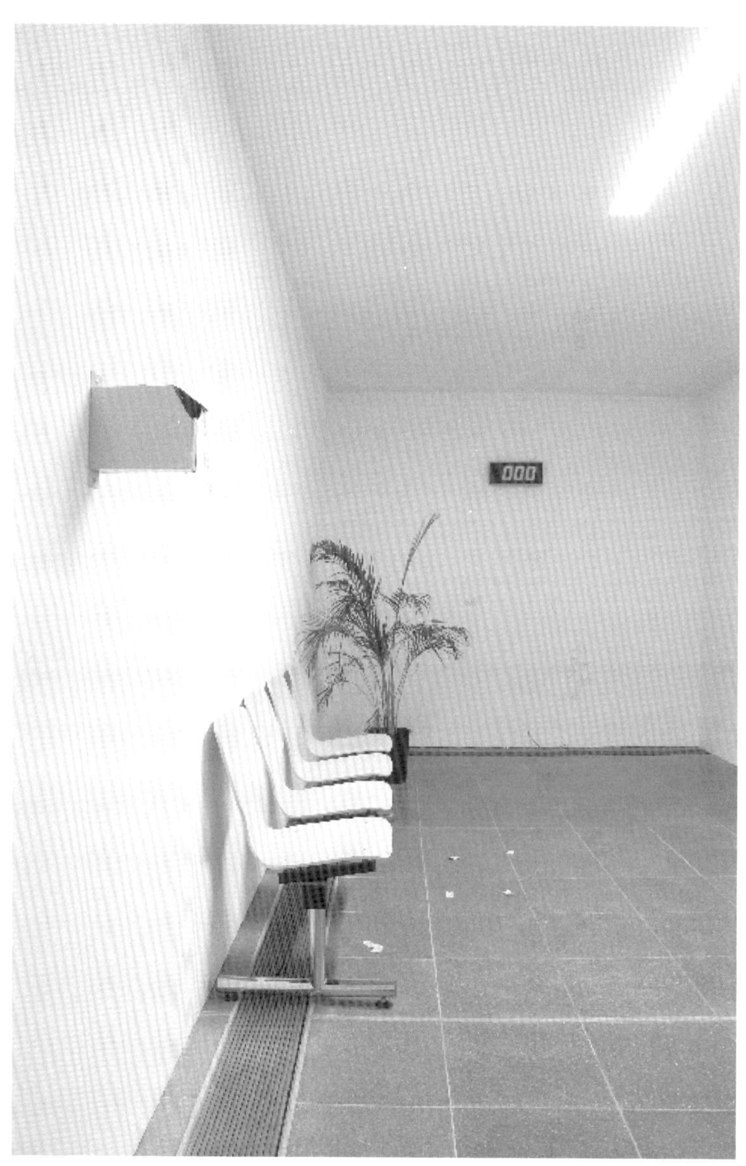

ill. 46
It's the Small Things in Life that Really Matter, Blah, Blah, Blah, 2006

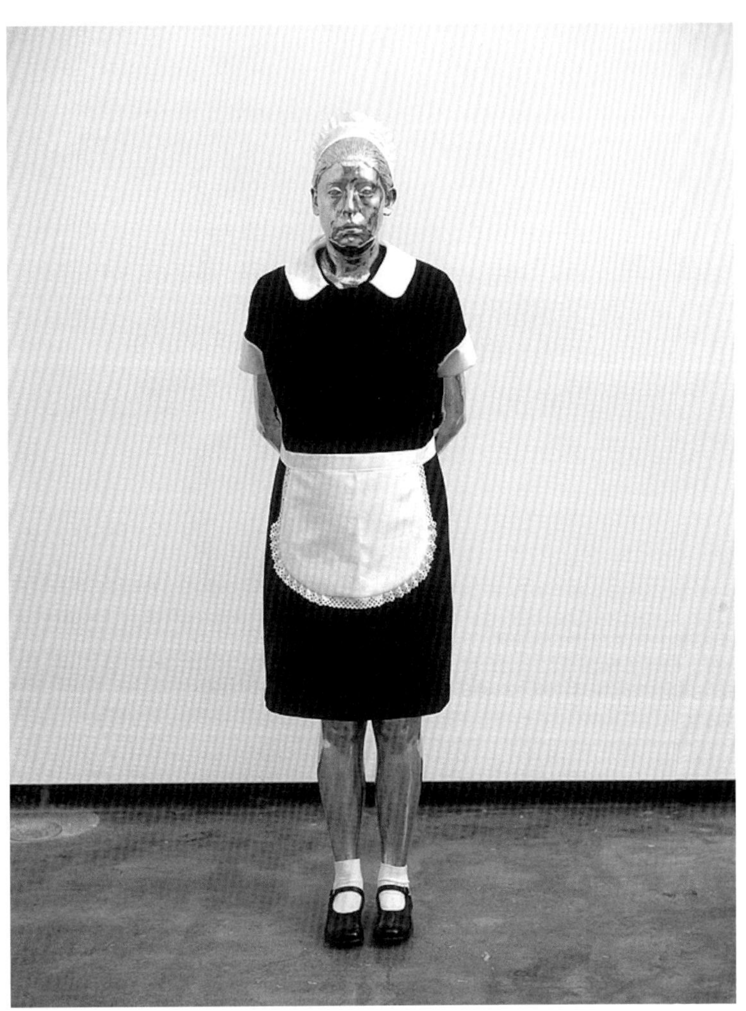

ill. 47
Rosa, 2006

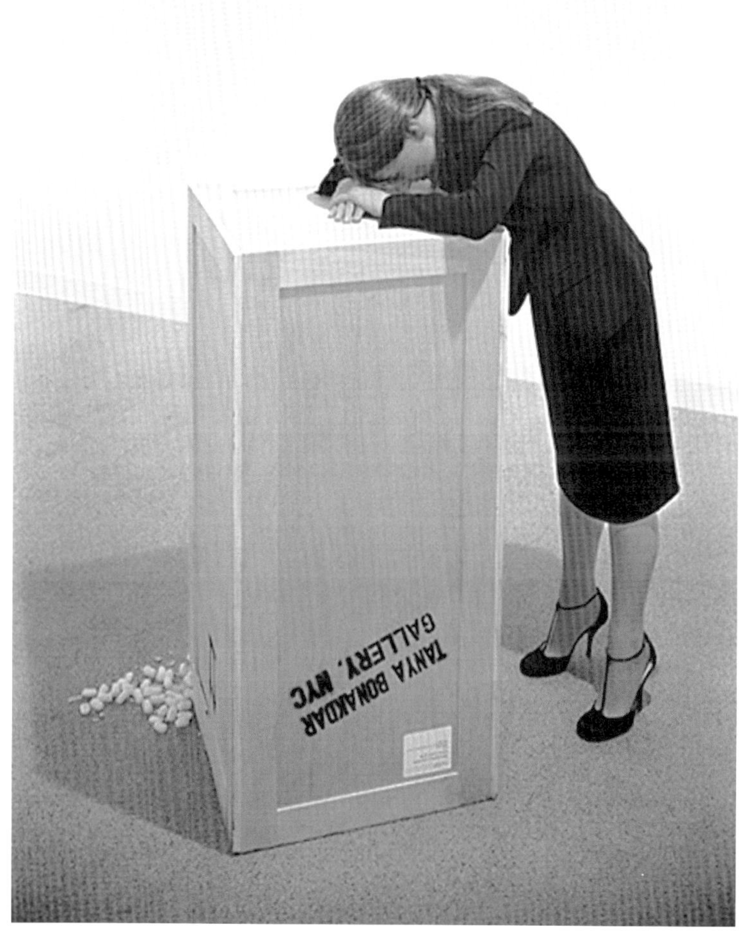

ill. 48
Tanya! Tanya! Tanya!, 2004

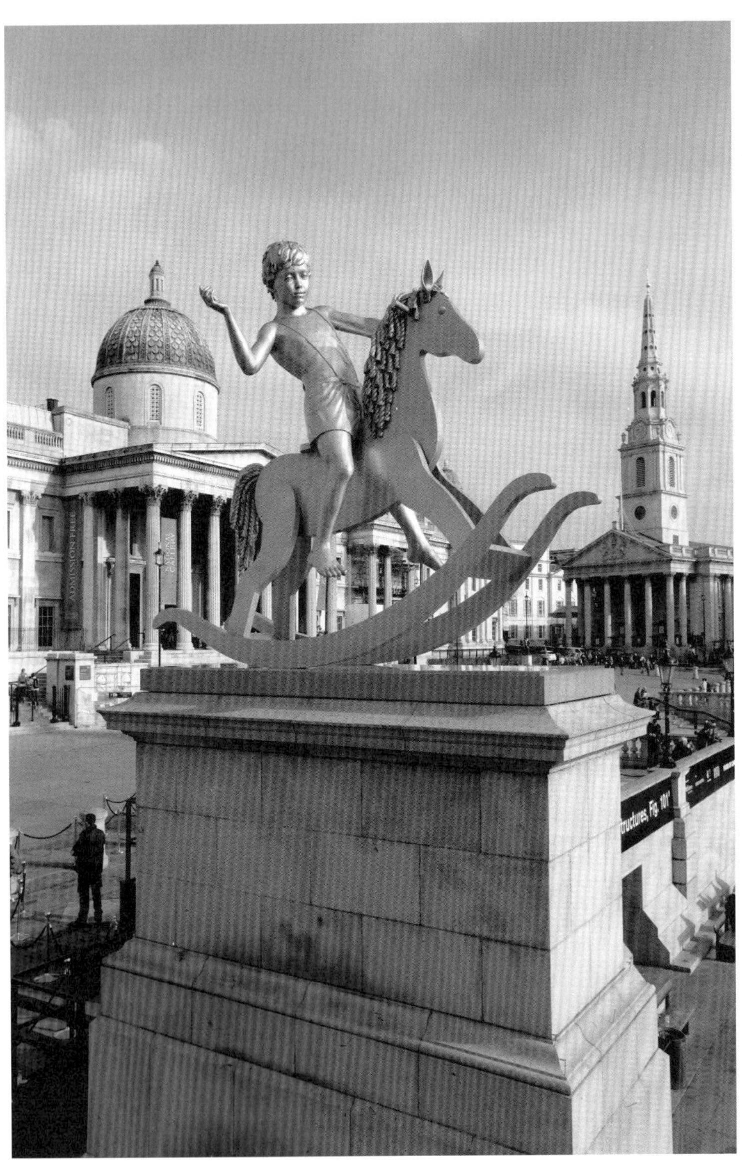

ill. 49
Powerless Structures, Fig. 101, 2012
Fourth Plinth Commission, Trafalgar Square, London, 2012-13

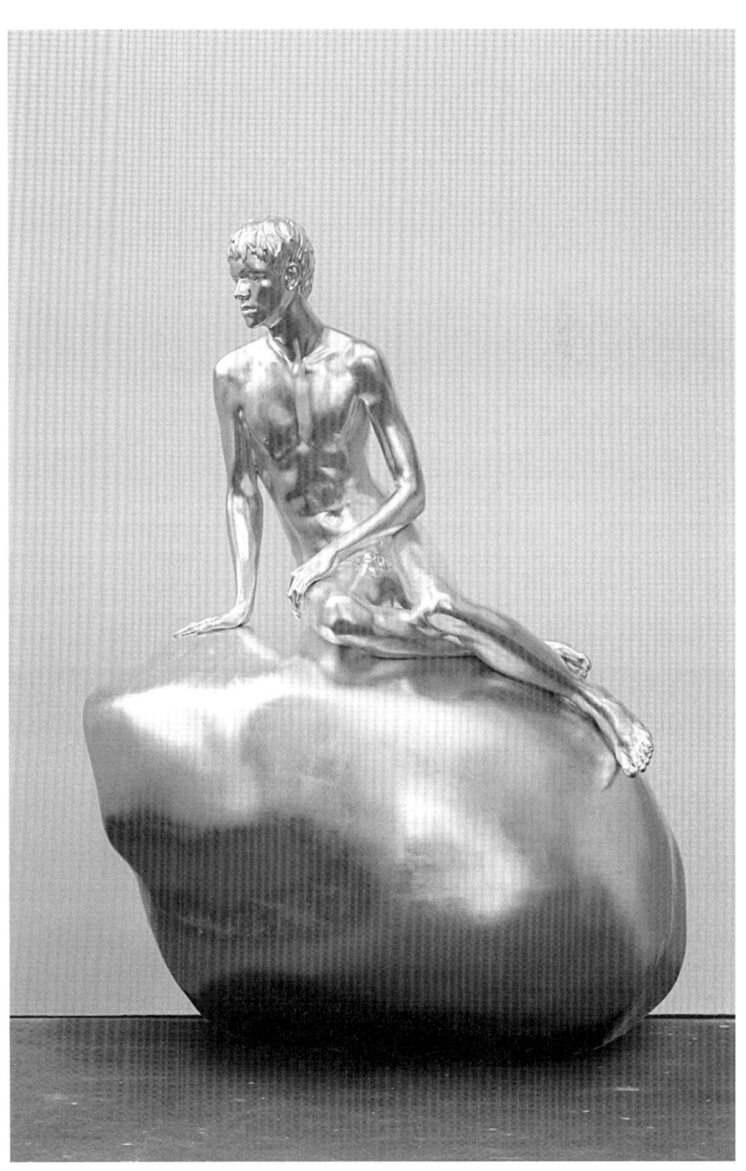

ill. 50
He (Gold), 2013

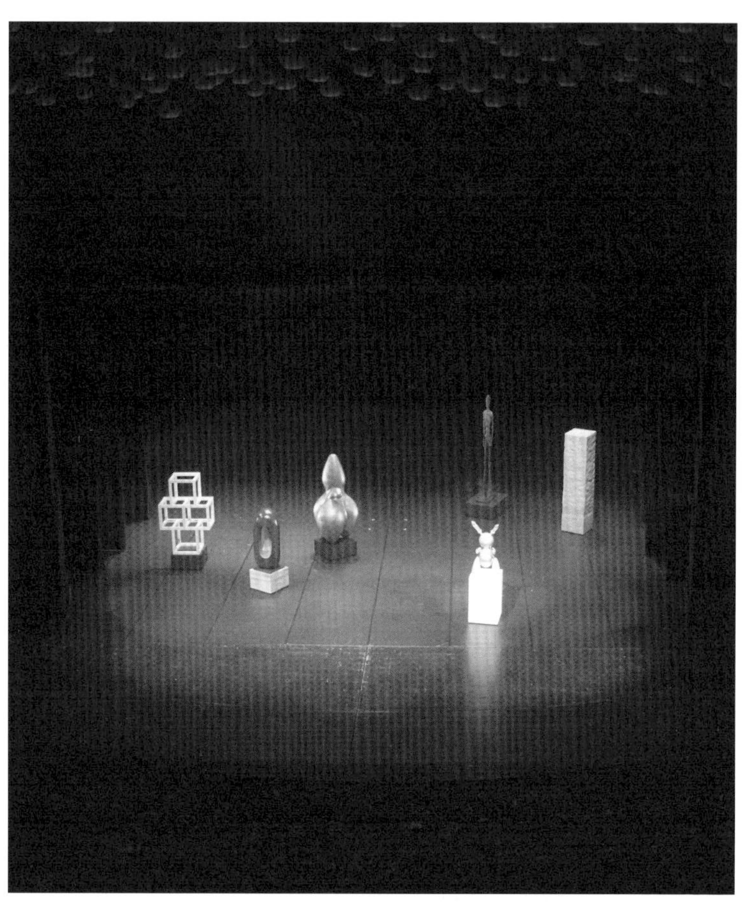

Drama Queens, 2007

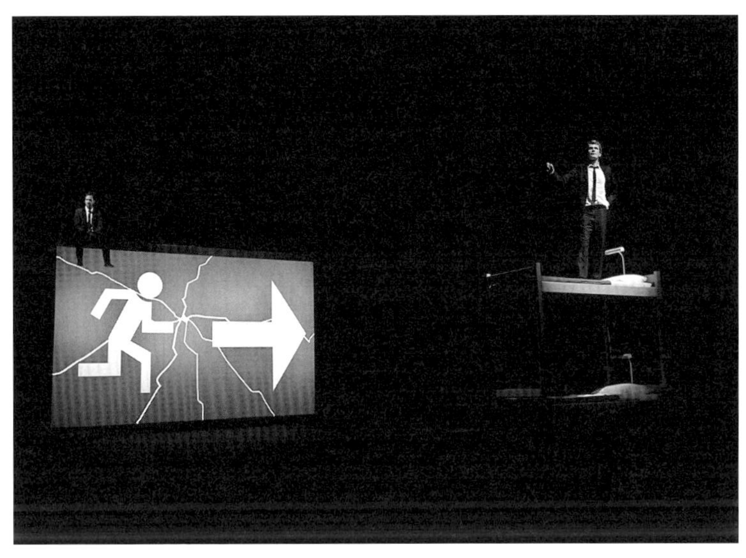

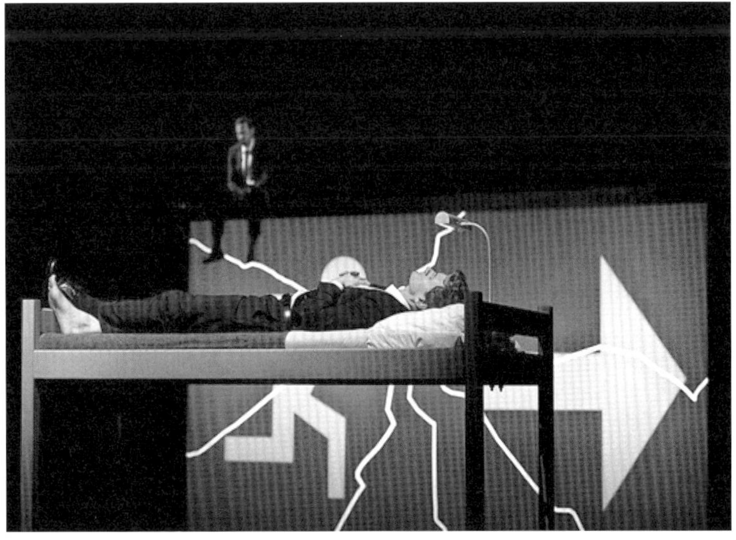

ill. 52
Happy Days in the Art World, 2011

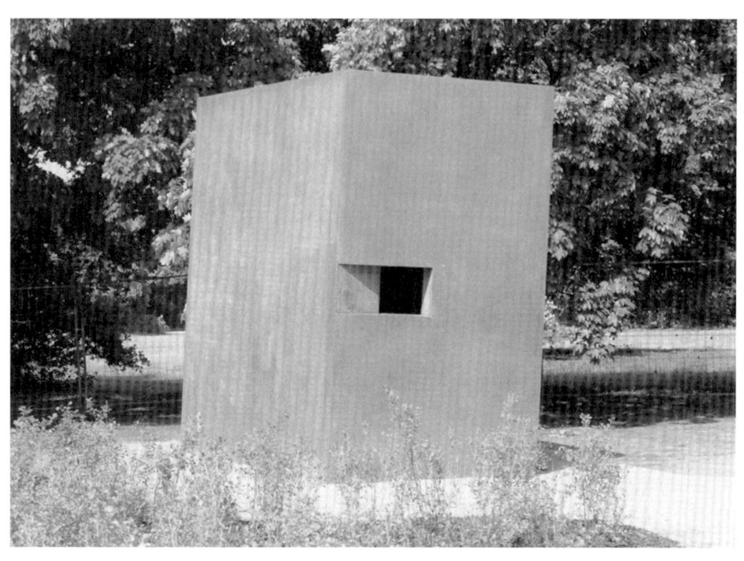

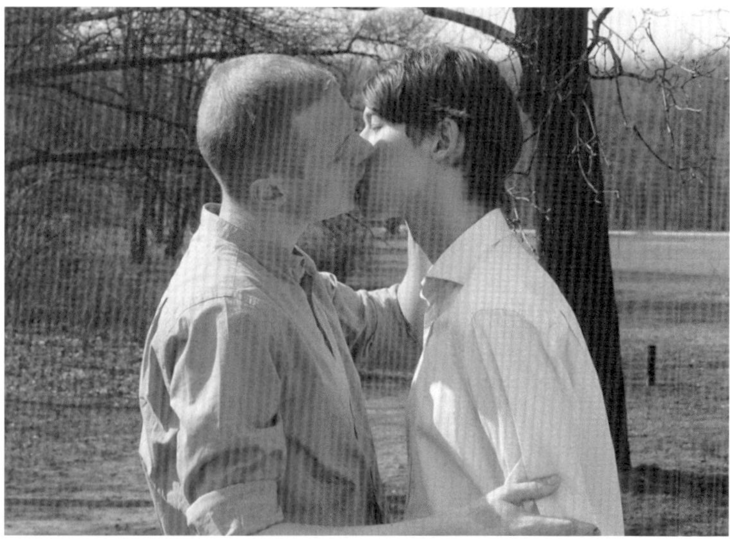

ill. 53
Memorial for the Homosexual Victims of the Nazi Regime, 2008
Tiergarten, Berlin

ill. 54
Memorial for the Homosexual Victims of the Nazi Regime (detail, video still), 2008
Tiergarten, Berlin

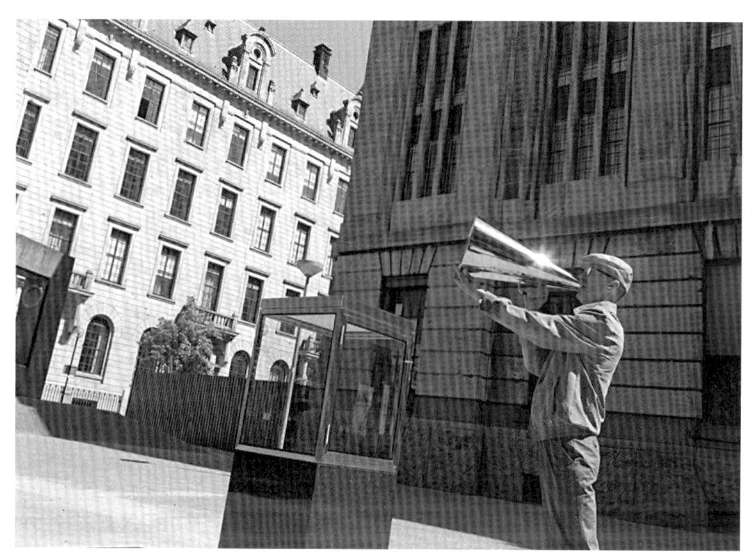

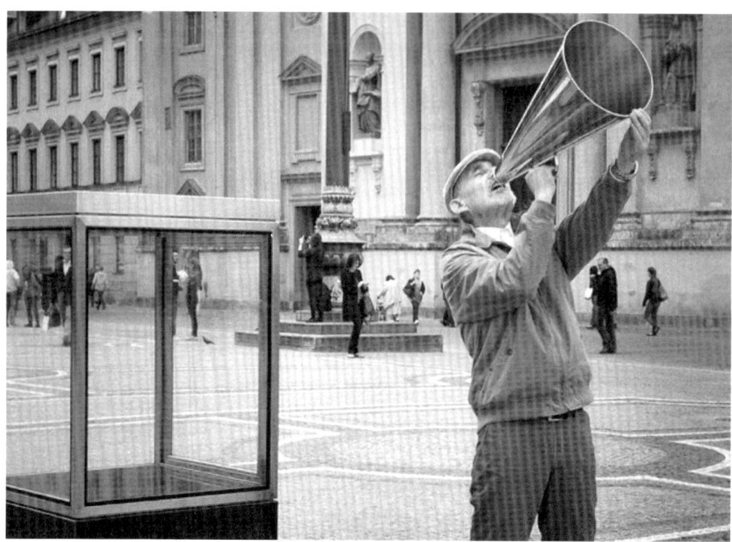

ill. 55
It's Never Too Late to Say Sorry, 2011
Sculpture International Rotterdam, 2011-12

ill. 56
It's Never Too Late to Say Sorry, 2011
'A Space Called Public', Munich, 2013

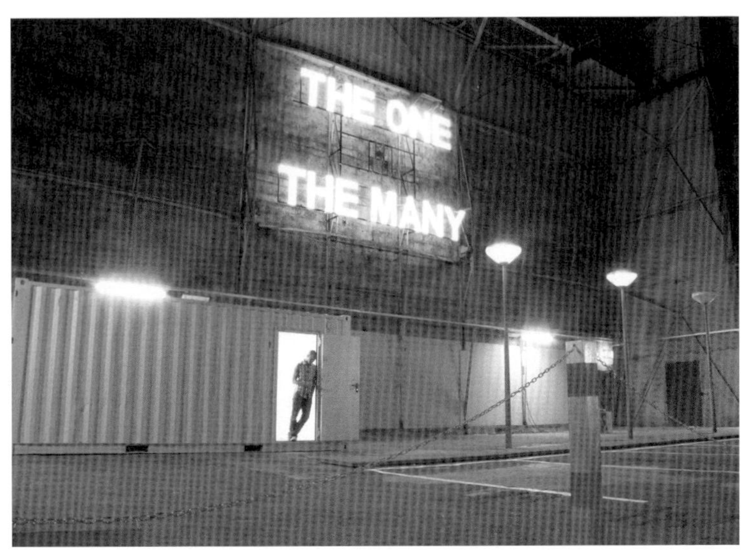

THE ONE
THE MANY

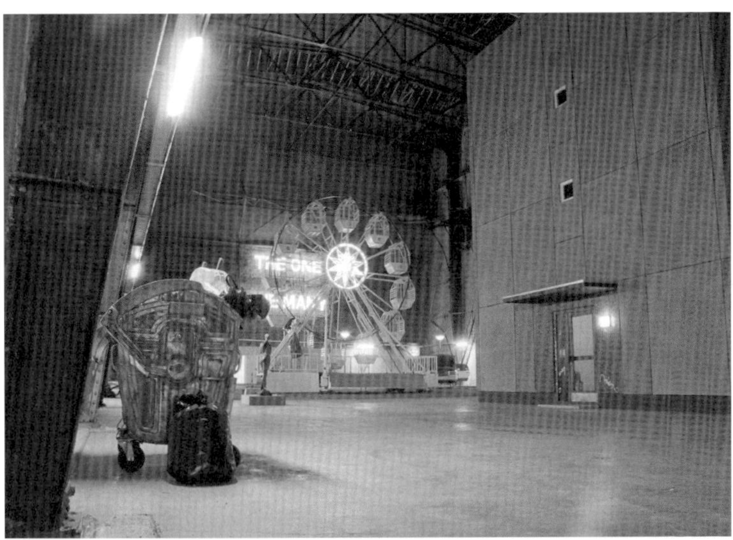

THE ONE
THE MANY

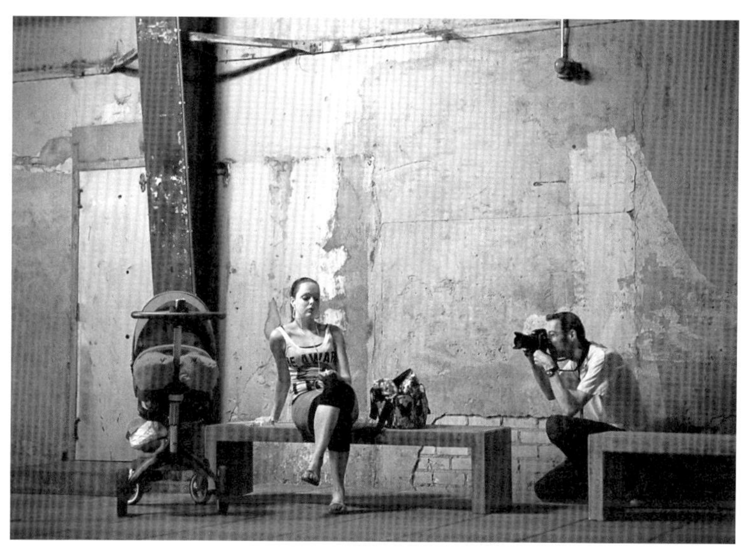

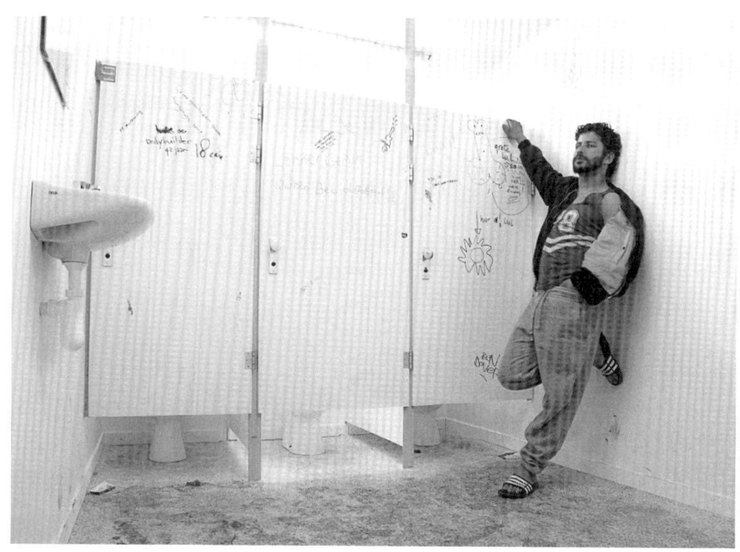

ill. 57
'The One & The Many', Submarine Wharf,
Museum Boijmans Van Beuningen, Rotterdam, 2011

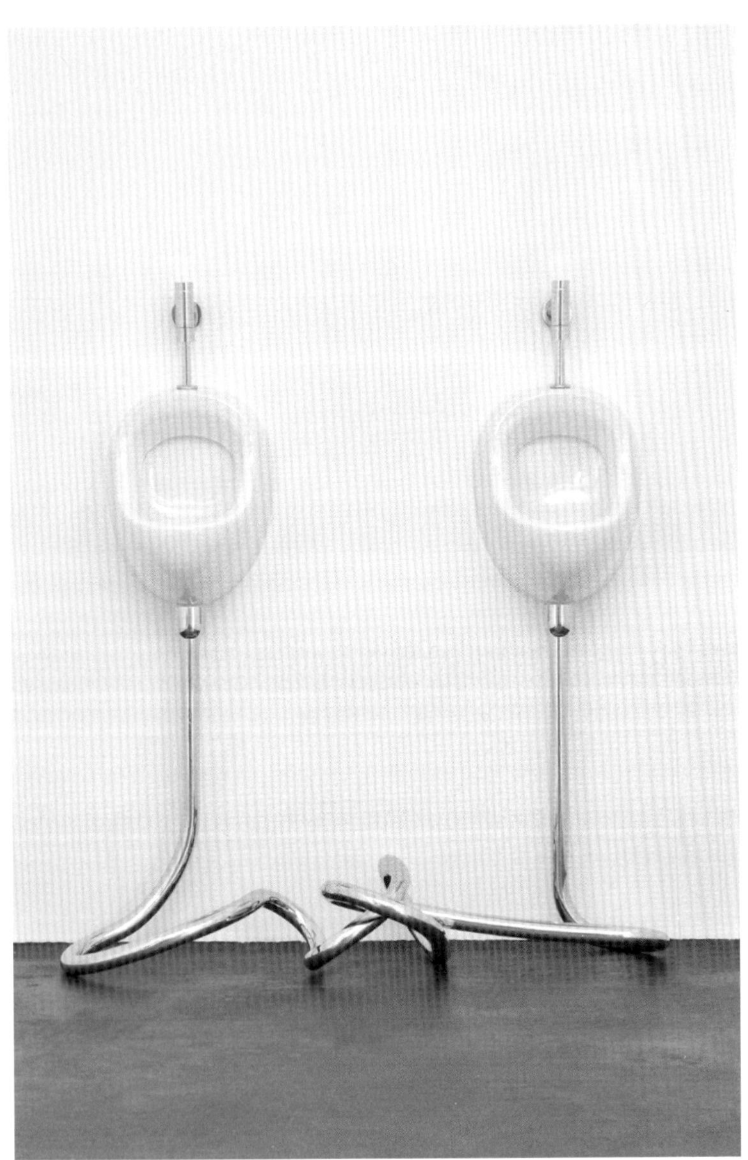

ill. 58
Gay Marriage, 2010

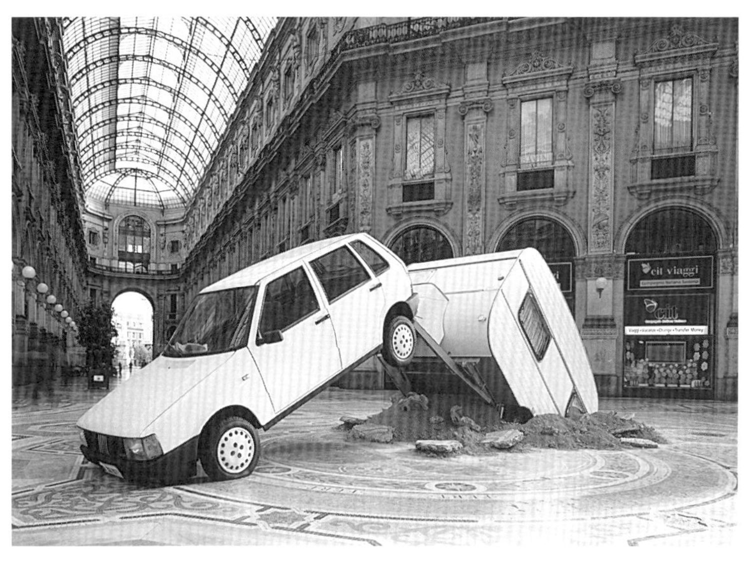

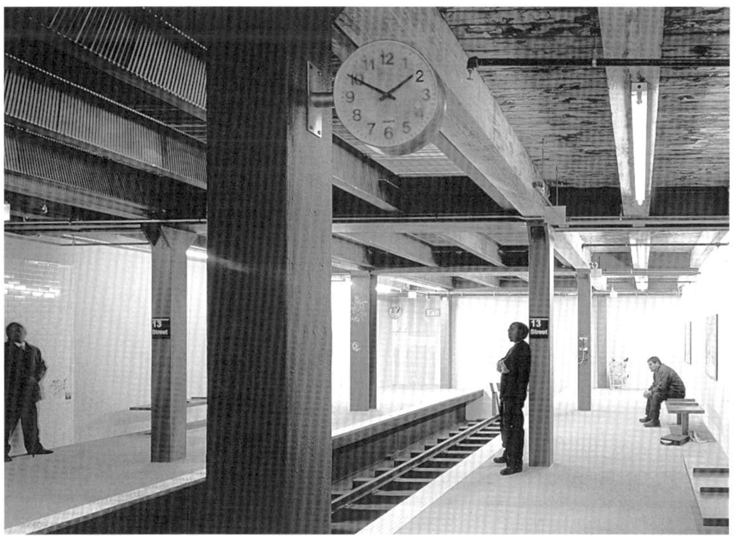

ill. 59
Short Cut, 2003

ill. 60
'End Station', 2005
Bohen Foundation, New York

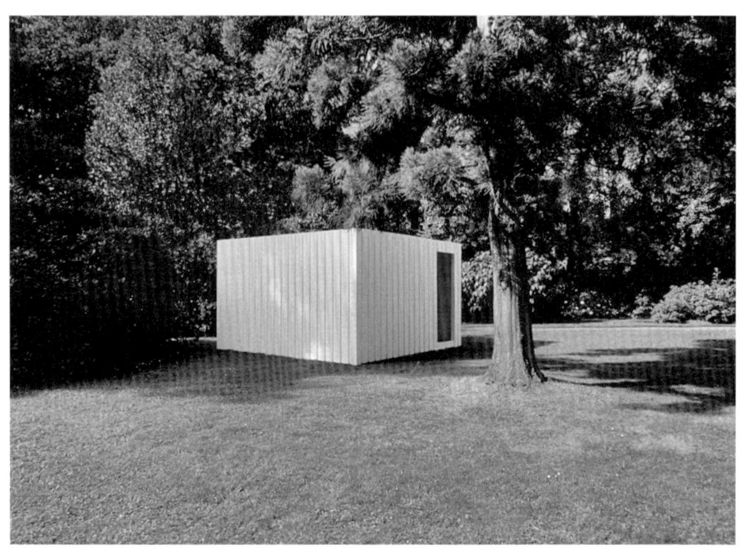

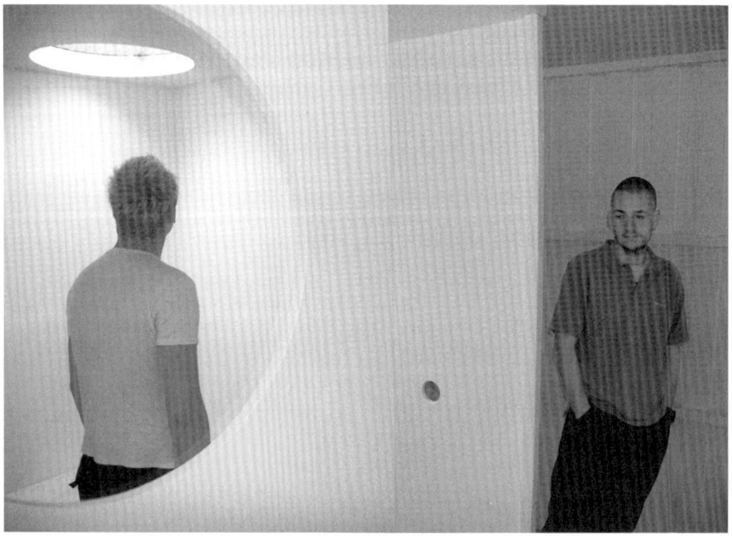

ill. 61
Cruising Pavilion/Powerless Structures, Fig. 55, 1998

ill. 62
Cruising Pavilion/Powerless Structures, Fig. 55 (interior), 1998

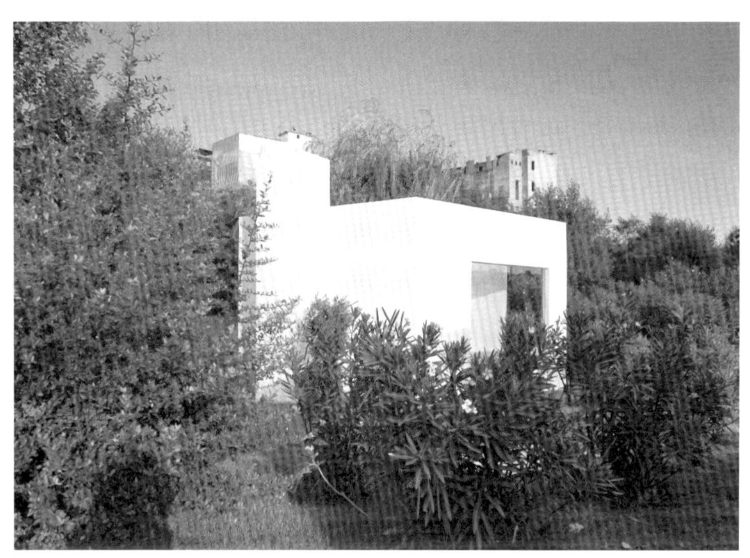

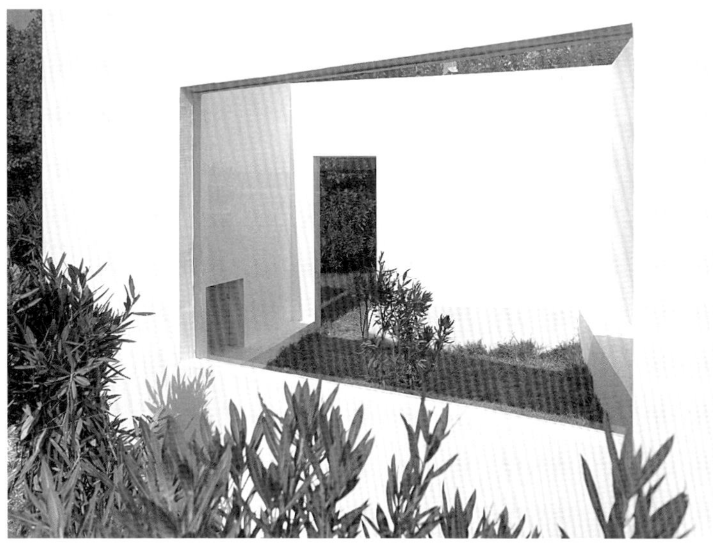

ill. 63
Use House, 2005

ill. 64
Use House (interior), 2005

Home is the Place You Left

ANDREW BERARDINI

You wait.

The bag, uncollected, endlessly carousels. Plonked there on the fanning, rubbery black conveyor belt encased in easy-clean brushed aluminum, it silently circles alongside the scuffed ghosts of luggage claimed. Leatherette valises and flowering carpetbags, monogrammed knockoffs and elegant portmanteaux, nylon backpacks and plasticky garment bags, squads of oddly shaped sporting equipment and orchestras of oversized instruments (battered sousa-phones elbowing nosy longboards), hard-body aluminum trunks and orphaned brown cardboard boxes, battered soft and swaddled in packing tape, bunched and frayed. Oblong, semi-soft black and navy roll cases, so anonymous they require besuited business travellers, dramimined and caffeinated, to double-check the long alphanumerics on claim tags to confirm that it was their single pleats and double-knits. Not today.

There's just one bag, grimed by the airport's shifty anxiety, spiralling forever. It's yours and you wish it wasn't. The contents aren't cute. No entry and no exit, the unclaimable interior and the consequences of its claiming: the humorless declaration of your right to remain silent, the Old Spice and yeasty flesh of the arresting officer as he acutely angles your arms uncomfortably against your back. The cool click of handcuffs and then the perp-walk across the repeating pattern of the beige and brown tiles through the Baggage Claim Area and towards the door marked with authoritarian typography 'No Access'. Every passing rubbernecker giving you the once-over twice, their stares dewing over with the thrill of voyeurism followed by complacent gratitude for the theatre of safety provided by law enforcement.

The contents if splayed on a criminal investigator's table would connect you to the ancestral manse of a troubled architect. You did not hear the sound of the shower. You did not hear the doorbell ring. You didn't witness the ghostly schoolboy huddled in an empty fireplace below his own portrait, the elegant furniture legging the faded carpets beneath chandeliers dripping with crystalline light or the glass-fronted cases neatly bookended with horse heads and vases, metal teapots and elegant statuettes, scattered heirlooms of other eras freighting the present.

You did not see the obsolescent beige computer and the stack of floppies, the rifled-through papers and stacks of unpaid bills, curling architectural drawings, draughtsman's contracts and rolled-up blueprints beneath the dusty models of failed utopias.

You didn't stumble by the half-filled boxes towered in the corner or the half-painted kitchen, spare white snowing over the curdled buttermilk colour that covers most of the house. You did not see the unmade bed in the mordant red bedroom, a perching golden vulture in the office, the faded rectangles paired together in the stale paint, or the scattered ashtrays with butted-out cigs and a half-smoked stogie, the grand piano cluttered with photographs of a boy becoming a man.

You did not hear the steady drip metronoming into the metal bucket from a leak in the moulding. You did not see the empty teacup on the veiny white and grey sidetable, a long dark teatime of the soul. You did not see the water flowing under the door. You did not hear the doorbell ring.

Minutes slump by, the carousel whirs on. A montage of waiting rooms and holding cells, heavy doors and sterile institutional corridors, court benches and long lines, cheap socks and creaking wheelchairs, bulletproof glass and neglected potted plants crumbling under smeary layers of recirculated dust. Legalese delivered by court-appointees, the definitive thunk of each phrase like the shutter of a penitentiary door. The administration lies just beyond the disintegrated staircase. A lifeless lunge towards an infinity of dullness, haze grey and poorly lit, carefully manned by the well-armed and casually cruel, fully authorized to legally administer violence.

Abandoning the bag and its future owner to their drab bureaucratic ends, you instead leave for the party.

Narrow alleys with curious stains labyrinth to a brick structure where a scripting neon buzzes *The Mirror* above a blue door with a torn scrap of paper clinging to its surface above a chrome mail slot.

Inside, a mirrored disco ball centres the dance floor like a crashed satellite, the light still playing against its surface refracting hazy moons of light onto the black walls. The red velveteen chaise-longues cluster around low glass tables littered with lowballs and plastic cocktail cups, ashtrays and crumpled cigarette packs. In the dim red light of the coatroom, a hundred empty hangers dangle uselessly, hanging only themselves. You peek into the bright light of the bathroom, where the pipes of two white porcelain wall sinks snake together. Two pairs of legs behind the stall hollow out an already empty club, the remains more lonesome and the possibility of communion so much further away.

Nothing feels right. Not its emptiness. Not the crashed disco ball spilling its mirrors all over the floor. Stagey almost, a set-up. You watch yourself as if you're watching yourself on CCTV, cheapish and grainy, news at 11 fodder for hold-up men with quirky styles or odd modi operandi. You watch yourself standing soundlessly at the edge of that semi-smashed ball, unmoving. You wonder when people watch themselves in moments of unguarded contemplation, if the watching reduces or balloons their self-consciousness. Does awareness make it worse or better? It is not the last party you'll be late to. There's another.

A plane and then a train connects to a bus to a boat bearing tourist couples clad in leisure attire, khaki cargo-shorts with large outer-pockets and salmon and melon coloured three-button polo shirts, DOT-reflective running shoes and zippered track suits with suggestive words stitched across the ass. You once envied the earnest embrace and perhaps unknown embodiment of cliché, a satisfying, if middling, place in a clear hierarchy of value. Everyone is splashed by a passing speedboat. The young euroteens with asymmetrical haircuts and synthetic quick-dry fabrics laugh it off. Their neighbour, an unreconstructed Reaganite, scowls and asks his thin, nervous wife, 'Do they still flush their toilets into the water?' The boat docks at dusk.

You weren't invited. A gap in the shrubbery lets you in and once in, no one could guess to hassle you. You wander from room to room, long cold views and high planes of crisp glass. Tree trunks rise through the living room and flow up through the ceiling, encased in vitrines like zoo animals, handbags. Best enjoyed by metaphysical exhibitionists, the future here is sleek and cold. So the pleasures must be messier, shit and piss and cum smeared across the sterile veneer of Case Study furniture, some approximation available in the stream of Soviet-era gay porn on a monitor tucked near the sunken bed.

Around the house linger only bored boys, lithe bodies taut with muscle and lank with repose. Placid and vacant, their faces do not invite inquiry. A small dog eyes the beheaded and unlimbed bronze torso of a young man, made sleek and pure: Brancusi's flight if only boys were birds.

The little dog does not move, you toe it with your shoe. Stuffed.

In muscular drawings and après-orgy snapshots hung around the house your eyes trace the blossoming cocks, unexpected tulips in a sudden winter bloom. On the desk, amid photographs and diagrams is an electric typewriter with a sheet of paper lolling out of it. Chapter one of a manuscript titled *The Erotic Writer: A Novel An Autobiography.* The first and only line typed:

A novelist is living in an exquisitely crafted modernist house

Like animal skins, six pairs of swimming trunks, three on top and three on bottom, sit behind glass in a frame. Stepping close to read the names, you notice a man in the pool. A bit older than the boys that populate the house, it's easy to imagine him the owner, the novelist. A white button-up shirt, his slacks rolled to the knee, though lacking in shoes and socks (those sit at pool's edge), his allover skin a soft-boiled pallor, he floats in the pool. Facedown. A gold watch and a packet of reduced-tar cigarettes rests on the bottom of the pool. Walking out to the edge of the water, you squat down, dip your fingers into the cool blue water. Tempted to poke the cold stuff skin. You don't.

You are escaping a bad love affair, a bad run, a bad feeling, a stretch longer than reckoning and deeper than can be admitted. You're not sure anymore who you're working for or why. The pitch and whirl haven't always been bad, the moral-compass wasn't always so spinny, but you ended up here.

The soft stench of a distant lagoon lulls over the far treeline, the meaty aroma of your own noisome corpus is unbearable.

Looking up you notice the neighbouring house and its open door. Looking back at the bathhouse of boys inside, you know without asking their answers about their erstwhile patron. Instead you stroll, casually but with purpose to the neighbours. Peeking in you see a knock-off Frank Stella and some elegant furniture, heavier, darker, the house of some haute-bourgeois family rather than the sex terrarium for an international playboy, however deceased.

It's best if you leave.

Other airports lead to other airports. Small pressurised rooms connected by long hallways linked by escalators, abstract carpets marched by suited men and women, vaguely militarist, faces marred with professional smiles but with skirts a little too short for soldiers and epaulets too stylish for officers.

As you come in to land in the oil town, an ocean away from the party, the city pustules out of the scrubby brown earth, crystal high-rises jagging up out of the miasma into the radiating blue of the sky. Distant cirrus clouds cast no shadow, rippling out in thin wisps, chem trails perhaps. You're escaping again, deep into the desert. A guy who knows a guy. In your econo-rental, you onramp onto the expressway and cut along the undulating curves through downtown. Beneath those crystal towers shimmering under a plumped afternoon sun, you can smell the plastic and BBQ sauce of their interiors.

Reflective letters on green signs point your hood this way and that along dotted lines, over cloverleafs and through underpasses, the numbered exits clicking off past developments advertised in the low hundreds of thousands. Gas, food, lodging. Waffle House, Cracker Barrel, Whataburger. The brown scrubland grows scrubbier, here and there an off-road cow holocaust exhausts steer shit and methane over miles of highway. Freeways curve into highways and tributary to byways. A desolate vast flatland horizons into an expansive sky, too bright and large to look at. The day boils down through afternoon and thickens into a gluey evening. In the smeary dusklight, you notice on the side of the road a structure like an unstained beacon. A clean, lonesome white building trimmed with black like coal frosting.

You pull over. The engine putters off. You get out to look. A few purses angle just so in the display. A shelved wall backlights shoes, all rights, pointed in the same direction. A sterile, minimalist white cuboid of retail, ladies' luxury goods. You try the door but it won't open.

Sitting down on its steps, all that was and all that was left behind fills the vast space between heaven and earth, lit only by the cool fluorescents at your back and the vanishing sun, totally alone in a way that feels like you always were.

A chortle catches in your throat, and instead you weep.

[ill. 1–8, 14–22, 43, 46]

The Erotic Frigidaire

MASSIMILIANO GIONI

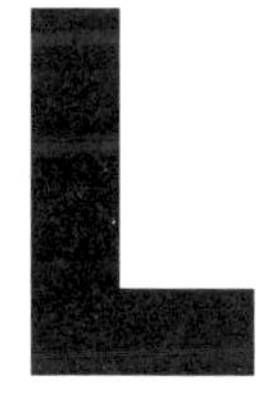

ove is a matter of spaces – a distance we constantly try to bridge even as we fear it might grow too wide. It is in this negotiation of proximities, in this crossing of territories, that we define ourselves as individuals and as members of a group, a couple, a family. Love dwells in the space between myself trying to become yours and you and me becoming us.

Elmgreen & Dragset – but I would like to call them Michael and Ingar if you don't mind: again it's a matter of closeness, and I cannot really be objective about them – Michael and Ingar have worked on spaces and structures, on architectures and buildings, often subverting and transforming their functions and compromising their distances. They have used space as others have used marble: the perimeters of a room, the walls of a building take on a malleable substance in their work.

They can be shrunk, polished, stretched and bent to illusionistic effects, but they can also float in mid-air, or sink underground. With their whitewashed surfaces, Michael and Ingar's constructions seem to mimic the repulsive, dull architecture of institutions – the endless corridors of hospitals, the waiting rooms of unemployment offices or the anaesthetised confines of some high-tech prison cell. There is something sanitised in their installations, a coldness that one is tempted to read as clinical, repressive or simply impersonal.

And yet all of Michael and Ingar's efforts concentrate precisely on forcing this distance, on warming things up, and one shouldn't forget that white is not only the colour of cold institutional anonymity: it's also the colour of bed sheets, possibly the tone of intimacy and sex. Split as it is between a playful, almost polymorphic sensuousness and a cold, impersonal rigidity, the artists' work speaks of a continuous struggle between proximity – or shall we say promiscuity? – and detachment. Could it be, then, that their fascination with space and the dialectics of public and private began precisely in that narrow passage we might call love?

Corridors, tunnels and conduits abound in the work of Michael and Ingar. Even when directly mimicking the architecture of galleries and museums, they tend to change the proportions of buildings and bring things closer, even a little too close. In their *Cruising Pavilion* [ill. 61–62], the geometry of traditional modernist architecture is fractured and partitioned to allow for unorthodox uses.

The interior space of the pavilion is a maze-like structure divided, segmented and then interconnected by so-called 'glory holes', circular openings and fissures cut into the walls for anonymous sexual encounters: the perimeters of the white cube suddenly activated by a new geometry of desire.

Michael and Ingar often depict a subterranean world that is directly connected to the realm of fantasy. Libidinal needs or romantic cravings are both evoked and denied in the melancholic *Wishing Well* – a square pool in the ground that is sealed with a glass safety lid, allowing no more wishes to be expressed or realised. But secret passages are reopened in 'End Station' [ill. 60], a perfectly reconstructed imaginary subway stop, in which time appears stuck in the early 1980s, when sexual voracity began to give way to the fear of HIV. In *Short Cut* [ill. 59], the artists imagine a mysterious journey through the centre of the earth by an eternally lost global tourist, while for *Dug Down Gallery* [ill. 40] they buried a gallery in the ground, rendering it useless. This is not so much a negation of functionality as an act of showing new possibilities, new escape routes, new knacks of continuing our old relationship with these familiar settings and designs – an art of both illusions and delusions.

Far from celebrating a conciliatory view of public space as a site for collective participation and reciprocal understanding, Michael and Ingar set up situations that are much more complex and conflictual. Their installations encapsulate diverse functions that are intended to generate intense frictions, such as in the *Cruising Pavilion*, or in *Use House* [ill. 63–64], a temporary structure realised in a park and left to be appropriated and misused by the different social groups that inhabit the area. In this way, they emphasise the fact that our public space is not a neutral zone whose main purpose it is to eliminate diverse identities, but rather a place where multiple cultural signs should be allowed to flirt or clash.

On other occasions, Michael and Ingar deliberately create environments that are based on some form of exclusion or denial. Doors are closed shut, stairs lead nowhere, pathways are blocked by obstacles. In 'The Welfare Show' – perhaps their most extreme exhibition to date – they created a total experience in which viewers were immersed, almost trapped, and forced to confront a series of dioramas and fictional constructions in which things seemed frozen, people paralysed, objects abandoned in a state of disrepair and malfunction [ill. 41–46]. At the centre of the show, a forgotten suitcase slowly turned on a luggage carousel, similar to those you would encounter in any airport across the world. Going round in circles like an unclaimed bag, 'The Welfare Show' operated as a mysterious bachelor machine, an onanistic construction where purposes were lost and gestures endlessly replicated, with no climax or release.

This grind between acute needs and prolonged frustrations is one of the most important stylistic characteristics in the artists' work. Their installations often encourage interaction and participation: they invite you or force you to need something – whether an object of affection, a touch or a sexual encounter. But once this mechanism has been set in motion,

Michael and Ingar – with a kinkiness that has something nasty about it – never really let you get what you want. In their work you are often left yearning for something that is constantly out of reach or kept at a distance: theirs is not an aesthetics of relations – it is an aesthetics of longings and desires. That's why their sculptures strive to attain a crispness and a clarity that flirts with the language of fashion and design: their objects possess an immediate optical appeal. They have to be seductive, only to make you want them more.

Glass walls, peep holes, mirrors and shining surfaces: these are just some of the devices that Michael and Ingar adopt to tease your gaze and amplify your appetite. This voyeuristic dimension recurs frequently in their oeuvre. It's certainly not a coincidence that in one of their most ambitious works, *Prada Marfa*, a perfect reconstruction of a Prada shop installed in the middle of the Texan desert, the glass doors remain locked. Michael and Ingar have adopted the strategies of the fashion industry, only to take away the actual moment of satisfaction, the purchase of the product. In a way, it's again just a matter of spaces and conduits: it's a tunnel vision that Michael and Ingar force you to adopt, as they titillate your desire to watch. At times, this optical fixation hints at sadism, as in *Somewhere in the world it's 4 o'clock*, in which we witness the slow and never-ending agony of a sparrow imprisoned between two window panes lying on its back, struggling against its fatal destiny. Also titled *Blocking the View*, this rather small piece in a large space reveals how crucial – and cruel – is the manipulation of vision in the artists' work.

Foucauldian descriptions of corridors, prisons and cells, the all-seeing gaze of the Panopticon, and its relationship to the mechanics of desire, all come to mind while navigating Michael and Ingar's spaces. Michael Asher's removal of gallery walls or Félix Gonzáles-Torres' negotiations with queer space and his desperate need to disseminate his work beyond the boundaries of the museum offer worthy precedents. But more than art-historical precedents or theoretical reading, I am reminded of Jean Genet's legendary film, *Un Chant D'Amour*, in which prison bars and partitions are literally and metaphorically perforated or transgressed to allow for sexual encounters and brief moments of ecstasy.

This longing for proximity seems to have found temporary fulfillment in *The Incidental Self*, probably Michael and Ingar's simplest and most touching work to date. Hundreds of photographs, snap shots and images stolen in moments of intimacy, transgression, happiness or solace compose a kaleidoscopic portrait of the artists that also stands as a humble yet decadent document of (gay) life in the year 2000. The photographs are lined up on a series of shelves – installed once again in a space that resembles a tunnel or a tight corridor. With the grandness of a history painting and the modesty of a family album, *The Incidental Self* reads like the letter of a lover bidding a last adieu, and resonates like a farewell symphony. But in spite of its confessional tone, *The Incidental Self* – like all of Michael and Ingar's best works – marks a space that is gently suspended between the infinitely personal and the dramatically public, a space in which the most intimate gesture is tied to a sense of social belonging.

The image of two men kissing in Michael and Ingar's Berlin monument for the homosexual victims of the Nazi regime **[ill. 53–54]** speaks of this very same blurring of distances, pointing to the moment in which the private takes on a collective, even choral breath. Again, it is just a matter of spaces – just a matter of love.

This text was first published in *Elmgreen & Dragset: This is the First Day of My Life*, Hatje Cantz Verlag, Ostfildern, 2008, pp.8-12.

Elmgreen & Dragset's Theatrical Turn

SHANNON JACKSON

In my dream we were successful *artists, we had something* big *coming —*
Happy Days in the Art World

On a blustery late morning in Rotterdam in 2011, a group of people assembled on a stone sidewalk near a defunct city post office. In front of this 'deaccessioned' civic space, an exquisite plinth and glass vitrine had been installed. Members of the group began to circle it. Some meandered; some laughed with each other; some photographed; some took video footage of people taking photographs. Inside the vitrine, a perfectly smooth metal cone shone in the available light, reflecting and refracting the images of viewers who peered at it. Near the top of the cone, a metal handle was attached, evoking the shape of a designer tool or household fixture fabricated for the Alessi consumer. More cameras and a larger crowd of Rotterdam's civic figures came forward to welcome assembled guests. As the clock approached noon, they formed an expectant circle around the plinth.

A bespectacled wiry gentleman in khaki and grey adjusted his flat cap and stepped forward to unlock the vitrine; he pulled out the cone by the handle, transforming the sculpture into a megaphone by raising it to his mouth. As the noon bell began to toll, the gentleman called out in international English, 'It's never too late to say sorry.' He spaced his words evenly and enunciated clearly, as if he wanted to make sure that all Dutch citizens within earshot were appropriately reassured. He then carefully replaced the megaphone, re-locked the vitrine, and walked out of the crowd and down the block. His gait and costume blended into the moving landscape of the city street as the bell tolled behind him [ill. **55, 56**].

To reckon with performance in the work of Michael Elmgreen and Ingar Dragset means reckoning with performance itself. Having collaborated together for over fifteen years, their projects have been contextualised by a variety of vocabularies, including terms such as 'theatrical', 'spectacular', 'exhibitionist', 'active', 'live', 'camp', 'durational', 'performative', and 'performance art'. The use of this eclectic performance-based vocabulary has also coincided with other artistic vocabularies drawn from Minimalism, institutional critique, public art, relational aesthetics and queer theory. What does it mean to extract performance-based work from the long arc of this duo's career? To what extent does this 'p-word' refer to a discrete genre of practice? And to what degree does it coincide with other structures deployed in their many sculptural, institutional and public projects?

Such questions are particularly opportune at a moment when a 'performative' terminology circulates in so many art-world contexts, one with a vexed and sometimes opaque relationship to words like theatre, acting, or theatricality. Performativity – with its distinctive suffix – is used to describe all varieties of contemporary art practices that seek, in Dorothea von Hantelmann's rephrasing of J.L. Austin, 'to do things with art'.[1] The term derives from a philosophical school of speech-act theory that focused on the world-making power of language. Its application in contemporary art expands upon the classical etymology of the word 'perform', stemming from a root meaning 'to furnish forth' or 'to carry out'. While all art practice arguably has the capacity 'to furnish' the world it simultaneously describes, some contemporary art is more self-consciously aware of its world-making actions. In Austin's *How to Do Things with Words*, such actions depended upon what he called the 'happy uptake', that is, enabling conditions for 'felicitous' reception that allowed the performative act to affect the thing it sought to do.

A piece such as *It's Never Too Late to Say Sorry* fits nicely into this capacious frame, employing, as it does, a durational and spatial structure that simultaneously seeks to reach, and potentially absolve, an unspecified addressee. We might then ask a follow-up question: how would the performative aspects of such a work interface with its theatrical aspects? A theatrical frame would focus, not only upon the audience's 'uptake' of a particular speech act, but also upon the casting, the costuming, and the blocking of the performer who raises a prop to express a script.

Such a focus would align with the etymology of 'theatre' as a term that derives from a root meaning 'a place for viewing'. The theatrical focus would emphasise, not only what is viewed, but how the act of viewing itself becomes a subject for reflection.

Odd as it may seem, the fact is that the vocabulary of performativity and that of theatricality are only occasionally brought into the same space. However, precisely because Elmgreen & Dragset have experimented so widely, the interpretation of their work requires an open and inclusive vocabulary. Indeed, the span of their work across genres of performance art, live installation, public sculpture, theatre and even opera provides occasion, not simply to document their hybrid practices, but more interestingly, to reflect upon the conventions we use to understand them. In what follows, I invoke different projects to track varied types of intervention, noting that structures of the performative and the theatrical appear in projects labelled 'performance art' and in projects labeled 'institutional critique' or 'public art'. I then turn to what might be an especially radical cluster of performative projects, precisely because their focus is so traditional: the theatre. I conclude with a return to *It's Never Too Late to Say Sorry* and with an anticipation of *Happy Days in the Art World*, positioning them as integrations and expansions of Elmgreen & Dragset's performative performances.

Expanded Performance Art

Such instant complicity … we were cross-peeing in a cruising park. Two steaming golden diagonals – Happy Days in the Art World

In many ways, performance was the form that brought Michael Elmgreen and Ingar Dragset together in the first place – well, perhaps the second place. Born in Denmark and Norway respectively, the two had varied backgrounds when they met in the mid-1990s. Elmgreen had some art training, wrote poetry and did odd jobs as an interior decorator. Dragset studied the Lecoq tradition in theatre school and also worked as a theatre instructor for children. After spending the first year 'doing nothing together but being boyfriends', they decided to begin collaborating. Dragset recounts:

> Since we had so many other things in common, and were getting along so well on most matters, we thought that we would try to combine my theatre experience and Michael's visual art experience … I started helping Michael preparing a show in Stockholm. That was because I could knit, and he wanted to do these knitted pieces: some abstract pets, that the art audience could hug and nurse and feel confident with … but in Stockholm nobody feels relaxed at openings, so we had to show the audience how to feel confident and how to use these knitted pets, and then everybody thought it was a performance – so it became our first performance … by coincidence.[2]

The coincidental turn to performance thus came about through an act of demonstration, a primary action aimed to provoke more actions in others. Whether or not viewers were moved to 'hug and nurse', Dragset's recounting shows objects being transformed into performance. The involvement of the artists' gestures before a group was enough to transform beholders into theatrical spectators. Because these beholders decided to receive the demonstration, not only as a performative invitation to act themselves, but also as an extroverted display, a lesson about the objectworld became 'a place for viewing'; the attempt to 'furnish forth' became a time-based piece of theatrical art. If the action 'was a performance', a shift in perceptual convention made it so.

Elements of this origin tale reappear in other early performance art by Elmgreen & Dragset. Dragset's knitting skills came in handy in a piece at the Institute of Contemporary Arts (ICA) in London in 1996, a kind of craft-based endurance performance where the artists unravelled and re-knit a 100-metre piece of white cloth for hours on end. (Appropriately, the piece was remounted in Paris in 1998 during 'Nuit Blanche'.) Incorporating the subtext of 'being boyfriends', the unravelled knitting was given an erotic transcontextualisation in another piece where the pair donned knitted skirts while performing in public toilets and soccer clubs; the unravelling of the skirt thus coincided with a camped-up act of seduction (1996) **[ill. 34]**. Other pieces made use of different theatrical elements. *Human Rights, Funky Hair* (1996) parodied the normalisation of gay parenting by dyeing a child's hair orange, positing this colour as the non-bio inheritance of the yellow and red lacquered into the hair of his temporary 'parents', Michael and Ingar.

This kind of self-transformation and self-costuming also appeared in *Untitled* (1995), which documented the two artists cross-peeing in a stream, wearing identical clothing and sporting bleached hair. The geometry of the 'golden diagonals' anticipated the doubled geometry that would undergird later sculptural projects such as *Powerless Structures, Fig. 255* (a transparent glass pavilion with two urinals installed back to back, 2003) and *Boy Scout* (metal bunk beds with the top bunk upside down, 2008). Most importantly, the captivating twin-ness of the duo in *Untitled* isolated one of queer theory's central theoretical challenges to psychoanalysis. Responding to the heterosexism of a Freudian model that separates those whom we desire from those with whom we identify, the boy-boy structure aligned an object of identification with an object of desire in a single figure.[3] In this piece, the person one wants *to be* is simultaneously the person one wants *to have*; 'liking' and 'being like' coincide in 'instant complicity'. Finally, the camera documented the event for us to recall decades later, a visual capture that reciprocally heightens the fleeting quality of the action. If the event 'was a performance', the camera retroactively made it so.

Early pieces such as *TRY* (1996) and *The End of Natural Behaviour* (1996) re-used but also extended this nascent theatrical vocabulary. Arranging beer and Walkman devices upon comfy rugs, *TRY* invited three men to bring in their favourite books and to relax in the setting. Titling the piece with a verb made the offer clear, obviating the need for demonstration. It is worth recalling that this piece took place around the same time that Nicolas Bourriaud curated his famous exhibition 'Traffic' in Bordeaux, an event that coincided with the French publication of *Relational Aesthetics* and the attempt to gather a variety of performative, interactive work within a relational art movement. *TRY* echoed Bourriaud's characterisation of relational aesthetics, for here, 'intersubjectivity' is the 'material substrate' of the art event.[4] In this case, however, that substrate had a queer erotics that gave the abstract 'relational' a heightened specificity, anticipating later works such as *Cruising Pavilion/Powerless Structures, Fig. 55* (1998) [ill. **61–62**] and *Untitled (Home is the Place You Left)* (2008), in which relational encounters have a distinct sexual politics. At the same time, the fact that those who 'try' will also be 'watched' joined participation and theatrical display. As a place for viewing that is also a space for connecting, *TRY* exposed the fine line that separated the extroversion of the theatrical from the relative introversion of the relational.

The End of Natural Behaviour brightened the line between the theatrical and the relational more intensely, returning to identical costumes and to semi-choreographed activities placed squarely on display. As the boy-boy duo performed their sailor routine, Art and Life playfully revised each other. Interestingly, the placement of this performance inside 'The Ark' – the name given to the Arken Museum of Modern Art's evocatively designed museum building – gave the piece a degree of site-specificity. By surfacing a queer sailor subtext within the museum's seafaring metaphor, *The End of Natural Behaviour* exposed and questioned the naturalised structures of the art institution. In other words, it was a performance that took a step towards institutional critique.

Installations, Institutions, Theatricality

We used to discuss Foucault and his 'Powerless Structures', the 'smooth spaces' of Deleuze and Guattari … We used to talk about important stuff. – Happy Days in the Art World

By the late 1990s, Elmgreen & Dragset's interest in performance art diminished. With the launch of a new series of works under the title *Powerless Structures*, they began to develop a reputation as practitioners of institutional critique, albeit a mode that expanded publicly and often entered into the territory of queer politics. Inspired by Félix González-Torres's practice, their connection to institutional critique came primarily from a fairly self-conscious decision to turn to the Post-minimalist geometries and formal interventions of an object-based practice.

'We were always curated to be the funny guys in the corner …[i]f some curator wanted to have a more light activity in a very stiff exhibition … [It was] very much like becoming a stereotype of yourself … So it was fun suddenly to do installation works, because that was a big surprise for everybody: "Oh they can do art objects!"'[5] Indeed, they worried that the gestic world of performance interacted with their sexual identity to fix them inside queer stereotypes: 'The performances we did were very important on a personal level and also on the level of artistic development for us; but you felt you were becoming too much of a gay icon, and that's where our *Powerless Structures* series started. That was also an emancipation from this stereotypical image of gay people or being a gay couple.

So we opened up our own artistic expression to include
all kinds of material, historical and cultural.'[6]

The 'all kinds of material' meant developing a stronger
relationship with the traditional materials of visual art
but using them to explore the material structuration of
powerful public spaces. It was at this point that they also
decided to move to Berlin to reorient their careers. In 1997,
Powerless Structures was launched as a series of related
spatial interventions where the autobiographical bodies
and identities of the artists were placed at a remove.
Acknowledging that the title 'is derived from our misread-
ing Foucault',[7] Elmgreen & Dragset began to explore the
reciprocal structuration of selves and institutions, creating
formal interventions within institutional structures in order
to propose new alternatives for inhabiting the world.

Even as we acknowledge the turn from performance art
to art objects in *Powerless Structures*, it is worth noticing
that performance-based techniques – both the constitu-
tively 'performative' as well as the explicitly 'theatrical' –
still animated many of these projects. *Twelve Hours of
White Paint/Powerless Structures, Fig. 15* (1997) oriented
itself toward the white cube of the gallery; like many
institutional critique projects in the late twentieth century,
it questioned the presumed neutrality of the visual-art
space by exposing its construction. In this case, Elmgreen
& Dragset painted, rinsed and repainted the white walls
of the gallery, positing 'neutrality' as a construction that
could be layered and removed. Interestingly, that construction and that layering required the action of a labourer.

Whether performing as artists who mimicked the house painter in 1997 or, with *Zwischen anderen Ereignissen* (Between Other Events, 2000) **[ill. 33]**, hiring professional house-painters instead, a critical stance on the museum gallery came about by exposing the labour required to produce it. Most importantly for the purposes of this essay, the attempt to expose the contingency and structure of the museum required performance. In fact, performance-based turns would animate several spatial interventions, including the artists' well-publicised decision to place an aesthetic umbrella over the construction and rehab process of the Kunsthalle in Zurich with 'Taking Place' (2001–02) **[ill. 35]**. Consider Daniel Birnbaum's extended account:

> When the crowd walked through the doors, they encountered a construction site in which two men were busy demolishing a concrete wall with sledge-hammers while another pair of workers were erecting a new one. Still another duo was removing the rubble and emptying the director's office of its furniture. The wreckage was everywhere and the noise was deafening. What was going on? Had there been an accident? Was it all a misunderstanding concerning address or date? In fact, everything was proceeding according to plan. What the crowd was experienc-ing and participating in was a performance piece, 'Taking Place', 2001–2002, involving six men restruc-turing an art center in the largest city in Switzerland. Why not put the office at the entrance to the building instead of hiding it in the back? the artists asked.

Why not open up the reading room and make it more welcoming? … The construction work, carefully choreographed by the artists, took place only when the museum was open to the public. After the first few days' dinof sledgehammers and concrete smashing, things quieted down. The show grew calm, approaching the solemn state we associate with the experience of art: The last weeks were about white paint, primarily; the very last days exclusively about degrees of whiteness and the fine-tuning of light.[8]

This project – like others by artists ranging from Hans Haacke to Mel Bochner to Andrea Fraser to Daniel Buren to Santiago Sierra and more – sought to expose the apparatus of the art world, sometimes through explicit revelation, sometimes through spatial re-organising, and sometimes by withdrawing, destroying, or rebuilding elements of a gallery structure. Interestingly, the act of infrastructural avowal in 'Taking Place' created a temporal experience. The exposure and reordering of the material space became a 'performance piece' that was not simply fabricated but 'choreographed'. The dismantling of the supporting apparatus of object-based art simultaneously opened the door to a new kind of time-based art.[9] A certain kind of cross-medium encounter thus enabled an anti-medium-specific gesture. For Elmgreen & Dragset, this gesture was another way to combine 'his visual art experience' with 'my theatre experience'.

Other projects exemplify a latent theatricality within practices of institutional critique and expanded public art. Several focused, not only on representing the labourers behind the construction of a public space, but also on the people responsible for maintaining it. The museum security guard is a constant if functionally invisible figure in most venues of artistic display. In *Reg(u)arding the Guards* (2005) **[ill. 43]**, Elmgreen & Dragset decided to call attention to this figure by defining a group of guards as an art installation. In a move that provoked reflection on employment practices within post-Welfare State nations, they hired unemployed citizens to be cast as uniformed 'guards', seating them in chairs within a single room of the museum gallery.[10] These performers both watched over the artwork and occupied the place of the artwork itself. Meanwhile, receivers faced sentient sculptures who looked back at them in return. *Reg(u)arding the Guards* thus conducted an institutional critique via a theatrical enactment that itself troubled who was beholding who in this place for viewing.

The exposure and deployment of an institution's latent theatricality appeared in several other projects that involved the creation of new character-labourers. *Tate Modern Walks – A Power Station Revisited* (2004) redefined the performance of the docent tour by giving spectators an alternative tour of Tate Modern's backstage and repressed history as a power station. The *Butler* of 'Celebrity – The One & The Many' (ZKM Karlsruhe, 2010) **[ill. 13]**, the *Amigos* of 'Amigos' (Galería Helga de Alvear, Madrid, 2011), and the *Real Estate Agents* of 'The Collectors' (53rd Venice Biennale, 2009) all adapted an existing labour performance to the needs of an artistic experience, choreographing gestures and rehearsing monologues that commented upon the classed experience of work and the classed experience of art in the same breath. Other works heightened the theatricality of the viewing relationship to reflect upon the menace and pleasure of seeing and being seen. The infrastructural intervention of 'Taking Place' took a more intimate turn in 'How Are You Today?' (2002) **[ill. 36]** when the artists constructed an enlarged peephole between Galleria Massimo De Carlo in Milan and the personal apartment of a neighbour above it. The female neighbour's everyday actions thus 'became a performance' by virtue of being watched. At the same time, the viewer's head appeared inside a large bubble visible to the neighbour, providing the opportunity for her to watch the viewer watch. Once again, an institutional critical gesture partook of a theatrical structure:

> You popped into her domestic setting like an alien … And you looked into this stranger's private life from a floor level perspective as if you were a bug or a frog … After having talked so much about 'the missing link' between the exhibition space and the everyday life taking place right outside its walls, it was such a great satisfaction suddenly being able to drill this hole into the ceiling – and by this simple gesture making a very concrete connection between the art space and its immediate surroundings.[11]

While some projects created surveillance schemes in which viewers remained relatively anonymous, several projects in-stalled this kind of reciprocal surveillance into their structure.

In *Paris Diaries* (Galerie Emmanuel Perrotin, Paris, 2003), for instance, young men were each seated at desks in a gallery and asked to write in their diaries for hours on end. When visitors entered, they could peer over the shoulders of the writers to read the journal, deciding at the same time how far to tread into private territory. Eventually, however, the diary writers began to record the behaviours and experience of the gallery itself; hence, when visitors peered over the shoulders of the writers, they suddenly realised that they themselves were being surveilled.

Theatrical Returns

As far as I can see, there is only a big black void like an endless darkened auditorium filled with a bored, exhausted, and invisible audience.
– Happy Days in the Art World

After several years of proving that they could make art objects with *Powerless Structures*, Elmgreen & Dragset began to recall but also expand some of their earlier performance art and theatrical interests. Of course, as argued above, such interests never entirely receded. Even as they were critically undoing and reassembling museum structures, they also took such infrastructurally critical practices to the space of the theatre. At the Odense Performance Festival in 1998, they created a piece that involved the de-installation of the theatre's stage and lighting equipment before an expectant audience. In *Erste Reihe (Front Row)* of 2001, they removed seats from the Schauespielhaus in Hamburg, replacing them with a large velvet replica that put the act of theatrical viewing on display.

Meanwhile, *Safety Curtain* (2002–03) positioned a huge vinyl eye on the safety curtain of the Komische Opera house in Berlin, questioning concepts of security and surveillance with its counter-gaze. In fact, in an art-world context, this kind of engagement with the theatre building was unusual. Most institutional critique positioned 'the museum' as the institution in need of critique, a habit that paradoxically legitimated the museum as the custodian of 'Art', even if the espoused desire was to question it. But if there remains some ambivalence towards the theatre as an institution – even if we are in the midst of a self-consciously performative moment in contemporary art – some curators and commissioning bodies began to offer new opportunities to stage a theatrical return. Elmgreen & Dragset jumped at the chance to do a set design for the Opéra de Lyon for *Faustus, The Last Night* (2006) and also tried out filmmaking in *L'amour de loin* (2008).

A far more explicit foray into theatre-making came about in their creation of *Drama Queens* (2007) **[ill. 51]**, a play that used a theatrical stage to comment upon the conventions and quirks of art-world behaviour. Conceived by Elmgreen & Dragset, with text by Tim Etchells of the British performance group Forced Entertainment, the play premiered at Skulptur Projekte Münster in Germany and then moved to The Old Vic Theatre in London with a celebrity cast performing the voice-overs. The play embodied as characters seven iconic artworks: Alberto Giacometti's *Walking Man*, Hans Arp's *Cloud Shepherd*, Barbara Hepworth's *Elegy III*, Sol Lewitt's *Four Cubes*, an untitled granite sculpture by Ulrich Rukreim, Jeff Koons's unstoppable

Rabbit, and a cameo appearance from Andy Warhol's *Brillo Box.* The text alternates between group dialogue and caricatured soliloquies that repeat art-critical statements as the internalised monologue of a sculpture. Says Koons's Rabbit, 'They said I was nothing, an empty gesture, a superficial, if kind of clever, decoration. Others said that I embodied a devastating critique of the economy of the superficial.'[12] The play thus puts a first person 'I' behind each sculpture who narrates his or her fraught history, loves, losses and merits as an art object with excessively egoistic subjectivity. In the text, Walking Man speaks with old-world weariness. Elegy III and Four Cubes flirt; Rabbit runs about the stage, recounting critiques of himself and occasionally getting the other figures to disco dance with him. The play ends with a silent cameo from the Brillo Box that brings an end to art-celebrity jockeying.

If 'performance' was something that Elmgreen & Dragset felt that they had to give up in order to be taken seriously as gay male artists, then the creation of *Drama Queens* marked a different kind of return to the form. This performance piece was wholly different from their knitting pieces, not only because it took place in a storied theatre rather than a 'gallery corner' but because it conformed to the conventions of a 'play' rather than 'performance art'. As a play, it used techniques similar to those recognised by theatre makers: script, proscenium stage, actors, movement and lighting. At the same time, it also recalled modernist art definitions of theatricality, sending up Michael Fried's anxious response to the theatricality of Minimalist sculpture.

(Fried famously articulated his anxiety with Minimalist sculpture as the scandalised encounter with 'the silent presence of another person'.)[13] *Drama Queens* heightened the threat by imagining that figure loudly talking to him. Meanwhile, other modifications made these sculptural interventions durable within the time-space contingencies of the theatre. The sizes of the sculptures were adjusted slightly to give them proportional stage presence as an ensemble. In order to provide a mechanism for motorisation, every one of the sculptures appeared on a plinth, with the exception of Untitled (Granite), who incorporated his own. With such plinths, the production both conformed to some traditional sculptural rules and broke those rules by making those plinths move. At the same time, the moving plinths neutralised whatever gravitational statement each had made in its time by equalising each artwork's relation to the raised ground plane of the Old Vic stage. While Cloud Shepherd had appeared on-stage in the Münster production, this character was cut by the time the work reached London, due to 'sightline and space issues'.[13] Apparently, its bulbous bulk could not be tracked mechanically by the remote or tracked visually by the hyper-frontality of a proscenium stage. What Etchells called 'a preposterous object-drama', another critic called 'The "Robot Wars" meets Samuel Beckett', expressing relief that it was 'not serious or snobbish, not political or peripheral, but clever and entertaining'.[14]

The extroversion of *Drama Queens* came into higher relief for some critics, who contrasted it with quieter 'living installations'. During the premiere of *Drama Queens*,

Elmgreen & Dragset installed another piece nearby entitled *Have You Come Here for Forgiveness* (2007). It consisted of a young man, perched on a short and squat plinth inside the Sprengel Museum in Hannover, reverently and compassionately handing out business cards with the title of the piece imprinted upon them. While in another context such a piece might have been perceived to be excessively 'live' or 'theatrical', the comparison with *Drama Queens* prompted critics to perceive it as 'placid and dry', a response that shows that the assessment of introversion and extroversion is highly relative.[15] In fact, the relative calm of *Have You Come Here for Forgiveness* was an intended component of the work. Elmgreen & Dragset hoped that this living sculpture would provoke questions about the values and affective affirmation that many seek when visiting an art institution, especially in situations where organised religion no longer provides a potent spiritual service.

The theme of forgiveness brings us back to where this essay began, standing before an unassuming Dutch citizen who boldly offered the possibility of forgiveness to anyone who decided to listen. Compared to the larger and more stylized 'The One & The Many', **[ill. 57]** which opened the same day in Rotterdam, *It's Never Too Late to Say Sorry* might also have seemed relatively 'placid' or even 'dry'.[16] However, the piece's site-specific and temporal parameters created (and as I write, are still creating) a performative structure with an intriguing durability and transformational capacity. After extensive auditions, Elmgreen & Dragset selected Wim Konings to play this role, an individual with a dual career as an artist and a postal carrier.

As a piece installed before a de-accessioned post office, the casting could not be more apt: 'The city had to close down the building', said an assistant in Rotterdam's sculpture project, 'because all of the mail systems are becoming privatized. Some think it might be made into a mall for high end shops.'[17] As Konings finished his announcement and walked down the block, heading firmly in the direction of City Hall, the piece begged the question: who needs to say sorry? And for what? Do civic leaders need absolution? Prospective retail owners? Dutch anti-immigration activists? Or the citizens of Rotterdam who are reckoning with their own relationship to imperiled public and civic systems? Interestingly, there will be ample time to consider different answers to such questions. The city of Rotterdam has committed to constant public reminding, authorising Elmgreen & Dragset's piece to be repeated each day at noon for 365 days. What might come of this ongoing act of public penitence? We can imagine that its content and its addressee will transform throughout the year, subject to more and less felicitous forms of uptake by the people who choose to listen and those who choose to ignore. The city and its citizens will contend with the happiness and unhappiness of 'saying sorry' as the conditions of performance change each day.

ID: We'll wait.
ME: Nothing more to add.

The premiere of *Happy Days in the Art World* at the Performa 11 biennial (2011) provides the occasion for this essay, and an occasion to survey a range of performative and theatrical work.

The play itself is its own survey, told from the biographical position of two-middle aged queer male artists who wonder what, if any, sense their lives have made. The title, of course, cites Sarah Thornton's widely-read *Seven Days in the Art World* while also corralling the central metaphors and figures of Samuel Beckett, a reliable go-to resource for existential reflection.[18] The play does not so much recall *Happy Days* and its buried female monologist as it does plays like *Waiting for Godot* and *Endgame*. Elmgreen & Dragset expose a queer male subtext in Beckett's familiar male pairings, transforming Vladimir and Estragon into ID and ME, who occupy *Boy Scout's* bunk bed and anxiously 'wait' for a new round of curatorial interest. Meanwhile, Beckett's classically contextless visitor is contextualized as BI, a 'SpedEx' mail carrier; BI is perpetually in need of a 'signature' and erupts into a jargon-ridden theoretical monologue that recalls the run-on monologue of *Waiting for Godot's* Lucky.

Samuel Beckett became famous as a playwright who broke theatrical tradition. However, relative to the performative offerings usually commissioned by Performa, this piece is quite strikingly 'a play'. More than any knitting-based performance art, more than the talking sculptures of *Drama Queens*, Elmgreen & Dragset's contribution is not simply theatrical, but quite shockingly 'theatre'. It is a script written by the artists, edited by playwright Tim Etchells and directed by Toby Frow. It has a set with props. It casts actors who play characters, wear costumes, memorise lines, exchange witty dialogue, and move about a stage space with rehearsed blocking night after night.

Elmgreen & Dragset have, of course, been creating sets, employing actors, devising costumes, exchanging witty dialogue and re-blocking the art world for their entire careers. With *Happy Days in the Art World,* they seem to be asking us whether 'a play' can be 'performance art'. In pondering the question, we might find ourselves realising that Elmgreen & Dragset have been making theatre all along.

This text was first published in *Elmgreen & Dragset: Performances 1995-2011,* Verlag der Buchhandlung Walther König, Cologne, 2011, pp.11-28.

[1] Dorothea von Hantelmann, *How to Do Things with Art,* JRP| Ringier, Zürich, 2010. See also J.L. Austin's classic, *How to Do Things with Words,* reprinted, Harvard University Press, Cambridge, 1975.

[2] Hans Ulrich Obrist, 'Performative Constructions: Interview by Hans Ulrich Obrist', in *Powerless Structures – works by Michael Elmgreen and Ingar Dragset,* Nifca, Helsinki, 1998, p.27, reprinted in this publication, pp.217-30. Online at http://www.nicolaiwallner.com/artists/micing/text1.html.

[3] For a queer critique of this psychoanalytic frame, see Diana Fuss, *Identification Papers: Readings on Psychoanalysis, Sexuality, and Culture,* Routledge, New York, 1995.

[4] Nicolas Bourriaud, *Relational Aesthetics,* Les Presses du Réel, Dijon, 1998.

[5] Obrist, op. cit., p.30.

[6] Obrist, op. cit., pp.31-3.

[7] Brian Sholis, 'Interview: Michael Elmgreen and Ingar Dragset', *Ten Verses,* 1 June, 2003. Online at www.briansholis.com/interview-michael-elmgreen-and-ingar-dragset/.

[8] Daniel Birnbaum, 'White on White', *Artforum,* April 2002, p.99.

[9] For more examples of how labour performance coincides with institutional critique, see 'Escape Artists' by Jens Hoffmann in *Elmgreen & Dragset: Performances 1995-2011,* Verlag der Buchhandlung Walther König, Cologne, 2011, pp.93-100.

[10] For a fuller analysis of visual art and performance issues as well as this work in the context of Elmgreen & Dragset's 'The Welfare Show', see Chapter Six of Shannon Jackson, *Social Works: Performing Art, Supporting Publics*, Routledge, London, 2011.

[11] Ivanmaria Vele, 'Elmgreen & Dragset: Boiler's Choice' (includes interview with Elmgreen & Dragset), *Boiler*, Issue 1, 2003, p.117.

[12] *Drama Queens*, a play by Elmgreen & Dragset with text by Tim Etchells, 2007.

[13] Etchells, 'More Drama', *timetchells.com*, 12 August, 2008. Online at http://www.timetchells.com/notebook/august-2008/more-drama/.

[14] Ossian Ward, 'Art Shows in Kassell and Munster', *TimeOut London*, 27 June 2007, n.p. Online at www.timeout.com/london/art/features/3089/Art_shows_in_Kassell_and_Munster.html.

[15] 'Michael Elmgreen and Ingar Dragset have hired an attractive young man to stand composed on a pedestal at the same venue, handing out cards to viewers that read (in English) *Have You Come Here for Forgiveness*. The duo's living sculpture is placid and dry when compared with *Drama Queens*, their profoundly funny, parodic theatre work staged for Skulptur Projekte Münster.' Michelle Grabner, 'Made In Germany', *artforum.com*, 15 August 2007. Online at http://artforum.com/archive/id=15678.

[16] For a lengthier account of 'The One & the Many', see 'Scenario Planning: Elmgreen & Dragset Queer Agitprop' by Aaron Betsky in *Elmgreen & Dragset: Performances 1995-2011*, Verlag der Buchhandlung Walther König, Cologne, 2011, pp.141-56.

[17] Interview with author, June 2011.

[18] Sarah Thornton, *Seven Days in the Art World*, W.W. Norton & Co., New York, London, 2008.

Ghostly Objects: When Forms Become Attitudes

BRUCE WILLIS FERGUSON

Suppose someone told a story and it went like this: a man named Abraham impregnated one of his slaves. The slave's name was Hagar and the son of their coupling was named Ishmael. Later, the same Abraham impregnated his wife, whose name was Sarah, and the son of their coupling was named Isaac. We now have two brothers – Ishmael and Isaac – issued from the same father – Abraham – with two different mothers – Hagar and Sarah. It is, as they say in comedy, a set-up. The plot thickens: the mothers are jealous of each other, the sibling rivalry begins and the punch line is coming. The story becomes more and more elaborate from that point on, developing twists and turns with the different authors who expand and adorn the various narrative productions. All of these emerging stories continue to be mutually intertwined, complexly braided, and eventually become contradictory, in multiple, mirrored and perplexing ways.

Importantly, this vexed, dysfunctional family tale proved compelling as a case study for three major religious impulses, each of which created its own differently inherited interpretation of the origin story. Versions of the same protagonists (the father, the mothers and the brothers) are central to each of these three primary religions' beliefs and orthodoxies. Each religion took the story and then expansively diverged from it over time, adding, deleting and shaping the plot and the characters to its own ideological and, eventually, theological ends. Each determined its own dominant emphasis as the narratives were told and re-told and then written and re-written and eventually enshrined in the 'holy' texts of the Koran, the Bible and the Torah. Institutions and even armies protect these keystone texts as sacrosanct, each faith secure in the knowledge that its version is impeccable and verifiable.

Thus it is safe to say that in this tale of a kind of polytheism, a class system at work, and the consequences of the forces of jealousy, greed and sibling rivalry, we have discovered a core narrative. However salted and thickened by each claim to authority, the same essential ingredients are basic to the texts of the three principal monotheistic religions. (It might be said that these three belief systems equally intertwine other common elements: the role of the desert as a controlling and dominant metaphor; the figure of Solomon, who plays a specific role in all three religions in significant ways, amongst many more examples.)

In the movie, *Rashomon*, made in 1950 by Japanese director Akira Kurosawa, we find a similar narrative echoing, although here it is developed deliberately and is associated with a much more modern sensibility than those that structured earlier religious beliefs. *Rashomon* is the story of the rape of a woman told through four successive and differing accounts from four witnesses, including the victim. The stories conflict to the point of complete incompatibly. Kurosawa embraces these narrative inconsistencies in order to articulate his belief in the subjectivity of such a concept as 'truth'. As in the *Arabian Nights* (a tale that can be described as both pre- and postmodern), in *Rashomon*, the facts are always deferred, denied a proper climax. The truth always lies elsewhere. The story ends with a nativity: the discovery of an abandoned child. The difference between fact and fiction, even fictional fact, is stressed, and the chronology of time is disrupted so that relativity is brought to the fore.

These two examples suggest at least one obvious conclusion: that different versions and even the same version of a narrative produce different responses and receptions. That is the nature of narrative and of narrativity (the state of inculcating the narrative). Narrative drives the story and narrativity is what we do with and to it. This is always the case, even when a tale is deliberately structured according to a strong plot trajectory and/or an overwhelming pedagogical or ideological message. We know from experience that readers themselves re-write the text when reading or telling it. Throughout history, meanings that were dominant and understood at one moment become contingent at another, while other previously lesser meanings move up to the pedestal in their place.

Or, when the context of reading changes and embedded meanings are loosened and unmoored, unconscious meanings float to the surface, becoming more persuasive than superficial rhetorical devices. A translator is always a traitor, as Walter Benjamin understood, pointing out the shared Latin etymology of these two words, and in fact all readings are translations since the receiver is never the same, even to him or herself. Jorge Luis Borges encouraged us to embrace the process by which the reader can rewrite the text, adjusting meanings to become more significant than perhaps the writer intended, or knew. Borges' tales produce incompatibility and ambiguity as consequential trajectories and are associated with a kind of 'magic realism', a term that could in fact be used to describe any tale, even those attempting to be scrupulously documentarian.

Bruno Betelheim, in his analysis of children's tales, was of the strong opinion that they shouldn't be illustrated. He argued very persuasively that to do so cripples readers' need to supply their own imagery to accompany the text. He believed that readers need to use their own subjective imaginations in identifying with these texts and merging them with their own desires and psychological requirements. A critique of Disney, for instance, would ensue from this approach, concluding that any imposed image of Cinderella or Snow White would be incapable of answering the desires and needs of a diverse global audience. The same principle could be applied to the problem with casting Tom Cruise as Jack Reacher (a midget cannot be a giant) and to why certain religions censure representations of God: believers need to imagine their own God, customised to their own needs, and not one illustrated by Holman Hunt, for instance.

That the correspondence between image and language might be dangerous has received further attention in the poetics of advertising and cinema; where images and text intermingle, these narrative devices can be either contiguous or contradictory, as Jean-Luc Godard has legendarily shown. We know that images and language, both in isolation and together, are used as rhetorical devices to persuade – to manipulate us as readers/viewers into understanding what they attempt to represent, even, as in Borges, when it is deliberately devious and liminal.

Art, which most often takes the form of images without direct accompanying texts, inevitably produces representations that themselves have to be read and re-read and their meanings adjusted. This is sometimes dramatic, as history and new contexts roil meanings about on the seas of change. Recently, Lawrence Weschler, for instance, brilliantly revealed the magnitude of the violence of the Dutch global imperial venture, found hidden within the small paintings of Vermeer. The wars of the late twentieth century became, for Weschler, the connective tissue with which to rethink retroactively about an age and a set of images that had for centuries been presented as serene versions of bourgeois comfort. Through Weschler's eyes we see a 'new' world of domesticity, with violence at its core. His proposition is that Vermeer's images conjure a picture not unlike the abiding genocidal ethos of the twentieth and now twenty-first century, where production is always only a step away from institutional violence or sweat-shop labour. As always, the peaceful images by Vermeer were made at the expense of death and injustice elsewhere.

Put simply, what all this means is that words – languages *per se* – and images – visual or material representations of various kinds of worlds – are unstable, contingent, uncertain, troubling, vexed and uneasy. Meaning is not assured and as Umberto Eco succinctly underlined, the same words that are used to tell the truth can be used to tell a lie. This oscillation of the function of language (and it is easy to see the same difficult wire-walking as a characteristic of images, objects, built environments and so on) from one pole to another on disquieting waves of doubt, is at the centre of debates on religion, politics and art. Because meanings are ascribed and arbitrary, rather than inherent, they are open to interpretation, persuasion, argument, and all the other devices of direction and re-direction through social means, technologies, media and disciplines of communication. If communication is our hope, as many believe, it is hope's dreaded doppelganger, fear, as well. Putin, Obama and other pernicious politicians are terrified that we might not believe what they say (and, of course, we don't).

Or in the words of Vladimir Nabokov – not a semiotician *per se*, but a philosopher of language nevertheless: 'Reality is a very subjective affair. I can only define it as a kind of gradual accumulation of information: and as specialisation. You can know more and more about one thing but you can never know everything about one thing: it's hopeless.

So that we live surrounded by more or less ghostly objects.'
And because Nabokov wrote in a second language (English),
he understood the traitorous nature of translation im-
planted in every word. Memory and desire (the past and
the future) are constantly affirmed and then contaminated
by spillage.

This fall, overflow, seepage from one state to another,
re-animated and re-proposed in an endless cycle, is one
of Elmgreen & Dragset's most iconic preoccupations.
The best example of this is their catalogue accompanying
'Home is the Place You Left', an exhibition at Trondheim
Kunstmuseum in which forty-five artists and writers
attempted to define the term 'home' with highly variable
results. 'Home' as a word is a brilliant illustration of the
way in which a single trope can be interpreted and re-
interpreted in a multitude of ways without any consensus
as to its meaning.

In the same way, 'loss' of power to Elmgreen & Dragset
is also a form of excess; it is shown to produce a symme-
try with power's abusive excess in the other direction.
On the one hand there is fiscal wealth, which consists
of the mind-numbing statistics of economists and the
accumulation of corrupted financial resources amongst
a small number of secular aristocrats – the artefacts of
capitalism and its believers. But on the other hand, there
is also a whole economics of symbolic labour and its
products that cannot be reduced to the mania of manna.
In other words, there is a conflict between the world
of money and its ghostly echo – symbolic capital.

Symbolic capital is what Pussy Riot, female performance artists in balaclavas, have in spades, despite Putin's military and fiscal power. Symbolic power is also what Nike has when it turns amateur sports into *de facto* professionalism through the dominance of its logo. Symbolic power is what Scarlett Johansson didn't understand when she opted to be a spokesperson for the illegal Israeli military occupation of Palestine rather than for Oxfam. It is not that symbolic power is less responsive than the power of capital to corruption or injustice, but it is an area in which anyone, rich or poor, can participate and possibly be effective. Art, for instance, is relatively unregulated, which means that it isn't subject to the same punishments that a fiscal economy inflicts on the poor and unjustly treated peoples of the world (the 99 percent).

Elmgreen & Dragset have discovered symbolic capital as a method of payment in the global structure: they are creators of material capital that exists as symbolic power in a world in which they are pointedly and proudly powerless (the titles of a huge percentage of their works begin with the *über* title *Powerless Structures*).[1] Their understanding of crime, for example, as an unlimited natural resource is one of the semiotic reversals that they pit against conventional knowledge, not merely as irony but as a kind of conceptual economy whose logic parallels that of the discovery of the unconscious – something to be understood as a form of vital energy rather than as a force to be repressed. As Nils Christie writes in the extensive government-style binder-catalogue for Elmgreen & Dragset's exhibition 'The Welfare Show': 'For all acts, including those seen as unwanted, there are dozens of possible alternatives to their understanding: bad, mad, evil, misplaced honor, youth bravado, political heroism – or crime.'[2]

This sense of the restlessness and the contextualisation of meaning – the way in which meaning swims and dives and disappears and reappears despite conventionalised institutionalised narratives that only serve single powers – is an added value in the economy of symbolic power. Elmgreen & Dragset's prisons, lying opened and upside down and sideways **[ill. 38]** strongly articulate the strange, ambiguous and arbitrary nature of 'crime' while opening up to unintentional homosocial overtones, like those that Jean Genet produced, in reversals of meaning.

George Orwell once said, 'Journalism is something that someone doesn't want printed ... the rest is press releases.' And this is the power of the powerless: to produce something that someone doesn't want seen in public, whether idolised, satirised, criticised or simply undermining the system of power's one-dimensional and authoritarian logic. And that of course includes humour, fun and danger, the most disturbing insights into power's slippages of meaning. It is not surprising, then, that it is in investigative journalism and in art that the systems of power are most deeply interrogated. Declaring artists and journalists (and of course immigrants) persona non grata is how the deeply embedded systems of power (left and right, since there are few differences in today's world) show their profound fear of symbolic power (the ironic 'powerlessness' of Elmgreen & Dragset's titles).

Despite billions of dollars spent on 'security', power is actually powerless in the face of newly created persuasive symbols of injustice (from graffiti to viral adaptations of politicians speeches to new icons of instability, to jokes, to unexpected images from cell phones etc.). As Ai Weiwei says, 'The government computer has only one button: delete.' But as he and thousands of others on the internet and in public squares throughout the world show, liberty can be suppressed on a global scale today. The need for liberty, however, seems to find new expressions in the economy of images and sounds in agnostic journalism and even more agnostic art. Activism is always, at the very least, symbolic power.

In *Spelling U-T-O-P-I-A* (2003), Elmgreen & Dragset play with science – the ultimate legitimising force in today's set of mythologies – and with cognitive science in particular. By isolating a chimpanzee in a space with sets of large blocks, each of whose six sides contains one of the letters of Utopia, they produce a large number of possibilities for the spelling of this word, even if by accident. It is a kind of 'Captcha' test of the sort invented by cognitive scientists, and the chimpanzee is an apt subject because it uses the same visual systems as a human being but is without language (as we define it). Elmgreen & Dragset challenge the notion of rationality by setting language in the abysmal space of a cognitive being that doesn't seem to need language, or perhaps does not need the notion of an abstract concept, to continue to function. In a sense, the piece speaks to the fruitlessness of many exaggerated claims to social- and hard-science experiments.

Science is of course as liable to the error of 'confirmation bias' as any other discipline, and can be made to function in the same way as any propaganda narrative. And Elmgreen & Dragset's piece has a Marx brothers kind of humour by virtue of its dysfunctional narratives, which illustrate the absurdity and pomposity of human behaviour without needing specific human targets.

Massimiliano Gioni has pointed to many of Elmgreen & Dragset's art-historical precedents: 'Michael Asher's removal of gallery walls, Felix Gonzalez-Torres's negotiations with queer space',[3] and has conjured the ghost of Marcel Duchamp by invoking their entire working methodology as 'a mysterious bachelor machine, an onanastic construction'.[4] And he is right to do so: a huge number of their works (the coupled trolleys, the distorted clocks, the idea of public spaces being made intimate and vice versa) seem to be an extended homage to González-Torres and are certainly an expansion of his sensibility, just as their doors are expansions of Duchamp's one strangely hinged effort. And one could as easily point to Matts Leiderstam's subtle re-historicisations of queer space, including genre paintings, or Bruce Nauman's unexpected spatial logistics and highly choreographed installations, or to a sense of humour shared with Maurizio Cattelan. But we can more simply just assume their awareness of this sense of a history, to which they are indebted as all artists are indebted; as writers are rewriters and so on. Although their work might refer to other artists and their legacies, it presupposes existing productive forces and enlarges and alters them, both in scale and influence.

Like Borges, they add magic to the historical message. They do not need precedents to give them legitimacy, as though art history were a legal case dependent upon proofs. In fact, the overwhelming number of works that begin with the word 'powerless' is a testament to Elmgreen & Dragset's renunciation of power that legitimises, even if such references by curators and critics might be meant as sympathetic. Elmgreen & Dragset use this 'art history', if it can be called that, as a point of departure; as a ground to their figure(s); as attitudes towards form.

In this way they can collapse or misuse expectations (their *Use House* of 2005 **[ill. 63–64]** is really a 'misuse' house for instance) and their *Short Cut* of 2003 **[ill. 59]** is not only not Michael Asher's caravan from Documenta but is an unexpected collision of a hyphenated car and trailer outside an urban Prada store, where the trailer has half disappeared. And that sets up the ultimate punch line of *Prada Marfa*, a Prada shoe store apparently closed for business, standing in isolation on a lonely highway in Texas. Here, the art-world *cognoscenti* come into contact with the snake-like line of criminalised nomads whose worn sneakers are a sign of the great migration to the North. The crosscutting of expectations is central to these moves, and it is often poignant, as when an animatronic sparrow lies twitching between windowpanes at Tate Modern, and is entitled *Just a single wrong move.* The wrong move, whether in a Tate window or on a Texas desert, is the difference between life and death. This is even more dynamically portrayed in *Count Down*, where explosives are attached to a safe door. One wrong move, indeed.

Here, loss is again at the centre of the deliberate movement away from power (which only accrues its own kind of emptiness through mass, as if believing that accumulation overcomes the unknown). Loss is the wrong move, by inversion.

It is powerlessness that propels the artists' sardonic sense of irony; a powerlessness that is tongue in cheek, since they have harnessed the power of many institutions to their will, but nevertheless remains the subject of their highly active and productive materiality. Or one might say that there is madness to their method. They present powerlessness as something anyone might have, or moreover, is likely to have. In this way powerlessness is a form of invisible accumulation – the forces and rights of everyone. Thus exhibitions like 'Home is the Place You Left', 'A Space Called Public', 'Taking Place' and famously 'The Welfare Show'[5] are sites of democratic discursivity; places where the language of power is usurped by the simple generosity of a space in which many people exhibit, talk, write and are given the power of the institution to use to their own ends. This fulfilment of powerlessness is of course powerful because the voices of many are heard against the fetishising of the voices and images of the few. Elmgreen & Dragset's power lies in giving up power; in passive resistance to the authority of institutionalised power, with its lies and its corrupt insistences. Instead, in small works, in installations where expectations are upended and ridiculously overcome, in strategic placements of images and figures, in exploitations of art-world legitimacies, in placements of fragilities and delicacies, in movements of deft anxiety, in collisions and collusions, they make the world anew, by-passing traditional agency and instead creating new agencies.

These are funny, serious and always conscious but without an agenda, or it might be said that the agenda is being discussed while it is in action.

The works of Elmgreen & Dragset might therefore be seen as illustrating the words of the supra-aesthetician Jean Baudrillard when he declares, in that French intellectual *haute* manner that is annoying but ever so smart: 'The absolute rule, the rule of symbolic exchange, is to return what has been given to you. Never more, never less. The absolute rule of thought is to return the world as it was given to us – unintelligible – and if possible a little more unintelligible. A little more enigmatic.' Like narrativity itself, the act of interpretation and mis-interpretation is encouraged against the sanctimony of legible injustices and normative signs. Family and home, science and law, and other pretences of stability, are underlined and their threads pulled apart. The invisible hand, so God-like in the hegemony of the neoliberal capitalist world, is, in the efforts of Elmgreen & Dragset suddenly seen instead as an authentic one-hand clapping, extracted from enforced and coerced reality in the name of solving problems that, as yet, do not have names. One hand, abrupt with attitude.

[1] Elmgreen & Dragset began their ongoing series of works entitled *Powerless Structures* in 1997. In this series, the artists re-examine various architectural, social and cultural structures. Past works have dealt with the control mechanisms embedded in the designs of public space and institutional architecture, and have investigated the desires behind domestic interiors and how these reflect and influence our modes of living.

[2] Nils Christie, 'Crime as an unlimited natural resource', in *The Welfare Show*, Verlag der Buchhandlung Walther König, Cologne, 2005, p.28.

[3] Massimiliano Gioni, 'The Erotic Frigidaire', in *Elmgreen & Dragset: This is the First Day of My Life*, Hatje Cantz Verlag, Ostfildern, 2008, p.12, reprinted in this publication, pp.153-9.

[4] Ibid., p.10.

[5] 'Home is the Place You Left', Trondheim Kunstmuseum, 2008; 'A Space Called Public', City of Munich, 2013; 'Taking Place', Kunsthalle Zürich, 2001–02; 'The Welfare Show', Bergen Kunsthall, 2005; BAWAG Foundation, Vienna, 2005; Serpentine Gallery, London, 2006; The Power Plant, Toronto, 2006.

Elmgreen & Dragset in Conversation

WITH HANS ULRICH OBRIST

HUO: Sixteen years ago, we recorded an interview, and soon afterwards your exhibition 'Powerless Structures' took place at Portikus, Frankfurt (2001). It remains one of your key shows. As Claude Parent said, we have a completely different experience in an oblique space, and here it wasn't even oblique, it was a hill. Can you talk about what triggered this epiphany?

ME: In many of our exhibitions we've worked with the viewer's perception, the conditions for perceiving the work. I remember speaking to you around that time about the rapid pace of viewing artworks in contemporary art exhibitions, and how this pace seemed to have sped up even more in recent years. People spend very little time in front of an artwork. We thought, 'Let's do something about that. Let's slow down the speed.' Portikus was a very significant exhibition space, but it wasn't big. So normally, you could pass through it very quickly.

By curving the floor upwards into a little artificial hill, we tried to create a sort of obstacle so that it would take a little more time to move through the space [ill. 37].

It linked to an exhibition called 'How are You Today?' that we did the following year at Galleria Massimo de Carlo in Milan, which was situated in a social-housing complex. The audience for that gallery didn't really notice the social context in which it was situated, and the people who lived in the upstairs apartment would never dare go down to the gallery. At that time, there was a lot of talk about how the art world should reach out to a wider range of people and we thought, well, first of all you need to get in contact with people other than the trained art audience. You need to say 'Hello! Welcome!' So we drilled a hole into the ceiling of Massimo's gallery up to the apartment of the lady who lived above, through her kitchen floor. (We got permission to do it on the condition that she'd get a new floor.) The only thing on display in the gallery was a simple ladder, and the hole in the ceiling. You'd climb up the ladder, and you'd end up sticking your head into her kitchen. If she was home, she'd look at you and wave, 'Hello!' [ill. 36]. We've often tried to twist and challenge the prescribed conditions of being a viewer, within the situation of visiting an art space.

ID: There was actually a second part, in a way, to the Portikus show. A couple of years later, in 'Spaced Out', we cut out the walls of the Portikus and basically left just the floor and the ceiling, so that when people entered through this wonderful, former library entrance, the portico, they came into a space where the 'walls' were actually just the surroundings: the adjacent social housing and a general view onto Frankfurt. So there were essentially two shows in the same institution, and both of them shift your perspective of what such a space means.

HUO: We first collaborated together in 1998, on 'Nuit Blanche' at the Musée d'art moderne de Paris, when you were still mostly doing performances. This was before the more participatory nature of your work had evolved. Last time, we spoke about the beginning of your collaboration, how you came from different fields, and how you found your own language. So how did the language evolve? After Portikus, what were, for you, the milestones or the moments where you pushed the envelope further?

ME: The Serpentine show was very important for us. And also two other projects of 2005, 'End Station' at the Bohen Foundation in New York [ill. **60**], and *Prada Marfa* in Texas. These were the foundation for a natural development that led to later shows like 'The Collectors' at the Venice Biennale [ill. **14–19**] or the last exhibition we did in London, 'Tomorrow' at the Victoria and Albert Museum [ill. **1-8**]. They were very much in the same line of thought, where we investigate the influence of spatial designs on our behavioural patterns as human beings.

At the Serpentine, we referenced various public or institutional spaces, ranging from welfare offices to hospital rooms to airport lounges, so it became one long, almost Kafka-esque journey through these rather sad and rigid interiors, using performance elements to speak about the human activities and conditions in each one [ill. **41–46**]. In 'Tomorrow', we created a private home, but this space can also be seen as some kind of indicator of changes in a city like London today, as well as changes in our culture in general.

ID: Many of our works that we did in the 1990s, and in the early 2000s as well, can perhaps be considered as rehearsals or crash-tests for what we did later on, where the works become more complex, or more layered. But all of them have elements taken from where we started out at the beginning, whether it was related performances, or these kind of physical experiments in gallery spaces and art institutions. Later on, these elements have all come together to form a new, more synthetic language.

HUO: The Prada project brought your work outside of the gallery space. Already some of your earlier works, for instance the Louisiana piece *Powerless Structures, Fig. 11* – a diving board penetrating a window – blurred the inside and the outside of the museum. But the Prada piece was sited in the middle of the Texan desert, and in this sense it was completely unprotected. It takes away our idea of the protection of the museum space, and that's something that I think also became important.

ME: It's important for us to allow ourselves to fail in different environments – not just in the art institution. [Laughs]

We always try to communicate in various environments, not only geographically but also in different professional fields, like testing ourselves in a theatre context, for example, with our play *Drama Queens* [ill. 51], or going to environments like the desert in Texas. The location for Prada Marfa isn't completely outside of the art context, because the Donald Judd Foundation is in close proximity, but it's different from doing a project in a space that's already defined by its context as an art venue.

HUO: Since 2001, you've become strongly involved with public art, most recently the Fourth Plinth Commission in London's Trafalgar Square [ill. 49]. There's also the project you did at the Tiergarten in Berlin, which is probably one of your most public pieces – it created a very public discussion far beyond the art world. Could you talk a little bit about the genesis of this piece?

ID: It started following the commission of the Holocaust Memorial by Peter Eisenman, which was initially meant to commemorate all groups victimised by the Nazi regime, but didn't really work out that way: it became an exclusively Jewish monument. So then other interest groups fought to get memorials for other victims, such as homosexual victims, the Roma, and so on. This took fourteen years, until there was a parliamentary decision to create a competition. Our proposal was the one that was selected and realised. We decided from the beginning that it was important to relate to the Holocaust Memorial located across the street, and to select imagery that left no doubt about what this memorial was for – not to go too abstract.

We also decided very early on to create a positive image within the memorial that wouldn't victimise today's homosexual population. Taking all these factors into consideration, we found a solution by appropriating Eisenman's concrete stelae and hollowing it out and then making a video to be shown permanently inside it, this eternal kiss, two men kissing, something that most people can relate to **[ill. 53–54]**. This ended up creating a huge discussion that went far beyond anything we'd ever imagined. It's a highly political thing to do a memorial about a historical event, much more so than just doing a sculpture in a public space.

ME: In your artwork you can play with representational images and values and push the borders, but if you do a memorial, there's a public demand put upon you to follow traditional representations. So I'd say that doing a memorial is almost not doing art – it's far more politically charged and beyond the creative process.

HUO: I spoke a lot with Félix González-Torres in the 1990s and he often talked about the 'desire for freedom' in the face of a very oppressive dimension in American society. He once told me that there was no such thing as a private space in the US for gay people. He referred to the famous case of *Bowers v. Hardwick* from 1986, in which the Supreme Court decided that gay men had no right of privacy, that the state could go into bedrooms and penalise men for having sex with each other. He often dwelt on these topics and, talking about the fight for freedom in America, he said he thought the role of the artist was something like an infiltrator.

A virus can be one's worst enemy, but paradoxically it can also be a model for how one infiltrates and then replicates within these institutions. It's a specific context, of course: he was talking about America in the 1990s, and you were working years later in Europe, but I wonder whether you felt, when doing this very political piece at the Tiergarten, anything in common with this idea of infiltration? Doing an alternative monument is another form of infiltration because you take something that's survived centuries as a format but then you somehow undermine it.

ME: It was tremendously important, what González-Torres did at that time, because it spoke about not playing the role of the 'Other', which of course had been raised as an issue by Judith Butler. That's very relevant in discussions of new materialism today put forward by Manuel DeLanda, and this whole notion of not being part of the system of binary oppositions. As a homosexual artist at that time, González-Torres made works that looked different from what so-called 'gay art' had looked like before. He addressed issues that dealt with homosexual identity, but through different aesthetics. Yet he was still allowed into the institutions, and in this way he infiltrated the highly conservative museum politics in America at that time.

Of course, a lot has happened in terms of identity since then, not only in relation to sexual identity, but all our various identities. They've been blurred. We're not working class in the same way we were decades ago. We're not artists in the same way as we were before. We're not gay men like we were before. All these identities have changed over time. And that creates a completely different starting point.

As a young gay person, you probably don't identify with works about traditional queer culture in the same way as you would have in the late 1980s and the beginning of the 1990s.

ID: And the consequence of that is that it's become impossible to infiltrate, in a certain sense. González-Torres disguised himself as a Minimalist, using the language of Minimalism to present very important subject matter: a political idea of a freer society. Luckily, disguises aren't as necessary today, since identity is much more fluid and constantly shifting, as Michael says. Identity is something that we've dealt with a lot over the years, especially after 'The Welfare Show'. In the exhibition series entitled 'Celebrity – The One & The Many' [ill. **9–13**] – which has nothing to do with celebrity – we address the ways in which the perception of the individual in today's society has shifted.

ME: Especially in London, celebrity culture is such a big part of the news media. People who have partly lost their personal identity as a member of a community, or a part of a certain class, are trying to live by the same criteria as celebrities who they only know through celebrity gossip in the media. Your quality of life is suddenly judged according to the standards of people who have completely different conditions, completely different life situations from yours. And that can trigger a deep frustration in your life because most of us, for obvious reasons, can't become the glamorous model or the actress with a high income living in Mayfair. Since González-Torres was working, the whole notion of identity has changed radically, along with the kind of parameters we use for evaluating our quality of life.

As a gay person, I'd say the biggest danger is the tendency for key elements of culture to become increasingly standardised. And that's something that we're very familiar with as Scandinavians, where you can see a total implosion of innovation, or lust for life, due to this demand that everyone should behave the same. You're accepted as an immigrant as long as you eat the same meatballs as everyone else. You're accepted as a gay person if you settle down in a nuclear-family structure exactly like everybody else. Everything is made to apply to everyone, no matter what. It's a cultural situation that you also see spreading out to other European countries. I mean, in Britain today, you're terrified of conflict; you're terrified of differences of meaning. And you want to harmonise everything. You want to have all kinds of cultural backgrounds and identities and beliefs and desires melded together into one big, grey ball of dough.

HUO: That leads us to something you said in our interview sixteen years ago: that 'identity is shifty'. And that was before the internet; now we have all these parallel realities, identity is a choice? Has the internet changed the way you work?

ID: Something that we've been dealing with for the show at Astrup Fearnley is a work that we started in the mid-2000s called *The Incidental Self*. It's a series of snapshots that Michael and I have taken over all the years we've been working together, and it shows a our life 'behind the scenes', so to speak. It's a kind of autobiographical, photographic series that goes on and on. But over the last few years, the perception of a work like that has become very different, because between the start of this work and now, you have the success of Facebook and Instagram and other social media, where people use this kind of imagery all the time. This is something that we have to deal with, but it's interesting to see how people react to a work like this today.

ME: It's a very analogue, old-school, classic, pre-selfie archive.

HUO: The exhibition at the Astrup Fearnley Museum will be like a homecoming, at least for one of the two of you, because it's your first big show in Oslo. Can you talk more about the Astrup Fearnley show? It's not a retrospective is it? It's more than that.

ME: It's more like new constellations of later works combined with earlier pieces, to see how they co-exist. The exhibition will also contain several whole room installations, environments that you'll only be able to experience fully if you actually visit the show. The physicality of going to an exhibition, to be present in a bodily sense, is something the internet can't give you. I think people go to art spaces far more these days because they need the materiality of things. They need the physical experience where they can use their senses, they can socialise, they can have an experience in real time in the art space, confronted by objects that are made for them to come and look at. The number of people interested in visiting these spaces that we call museums, and kunsthalles and galleries, is increasing because they need something else in their lives other than the 2D reality in front of the screen.

ID: And the title is 'Biography'. And I would say that the way we deal with this term is inspired by the internet era, in the sense that the internet has contributed so much to the way we now realise the fiction of history, the fiction of identity, the fiction of culture, the fiction of any biography. We know it's not necessarily objective or true, but we still get our information from the internet.

HUO: The show will be in the new Renzo Piano building of the Astrup Fearnley Museet **[ill. 26]**?

ID: Thank you, Renzo Piano, for the challenge! [Laughter]

ME: It's not a *Gesamtkunstwerk*, but as always when we do an exhibition, we also consider the exhibition format as an artwork. It's not that the exhibition is just the sum of different artworks. That sum of different artworks is an artwork in itself. For us, since we're not big believers in masterpieces that say the same thing no matter what context they're presented in, it's like giving the single artworks a completely new life, a completely new challenge, by placing them in different arrangements, in new contexts, in new environments that we build up for them.
We'll also restage an exhibition called 'Too Late' that we initially did at the Victoria Miro Gallery, London, in 2008 **[ill. 20–22]**. It coincided exactly with the big credit crunch, so the title gained a different, ironic twist. But the installation itself was actually a club that was closed down, where the party had already taken place – visitors just saw the remains of a party from the night before.

We like these ideas about the before-life of an exhibition and the afterlife of an exhibition.

HUO: The museum has long been a muse for artists. You've just done this exhibition 'Tomorrow' at the Victoria and Albert Museum, which is inspired by the objects in the museum itself. Would you say that the museum is your muse?

ID: Well, the Victoria and Albert exhibition was very much a once-in-a-lifetime opportunity, because the museum is so unique. The collection has a non-hierarchical structure in terms of the objects amassed. There are many, many inspiring things within that museum that brought us to construct this mixture that we like, of architecture, design and antiques versus contemporary art objects. And it also gave us the opportunity to give a life back to these objects in the museum, a life that they were initially intended to have. Objects are normally placed in vitrines or on pedestals, but that's not really where they belong. They belong in a home. And that's what we did. We created a home inside the museum.

ME: The Victoria and Albert collection is quite random. It has everything from masterpieces to things that you could find in a thrift store. It's based on private collections donated to the museum, so it's not objective in any way. It's not scientific. It's not historically correct. This personal approach inspired us to do something like a private home in the museum to emphasise that it's always a subjective matter to do exhibitions.

Fortunately, artists and curators are human beings, and all their weird desires and neuroses influence what will be on display.

ID: The V&A has a lot of replicas in its collection and this is also something that inspires us. We've often done replicas ourselves – whether a Brancusi sculpture or a Prada boutique. And when we alter, add other elements, or displace such objects or entities, we're curious to see what happens. It's a constant research process.

ME: Most artworks or antiques also depend on the context within which they're presented. Are they in a vitrine in a white-walled space or are they shown in a private setting? What are these objects' histories? What are their backgrounds? What were they made for? And what were their biographies, their trajectory to becoming an object in a museum?

HUO: Finally, I'd like to ask about your unrealised projects. It's the only recurring question in all my interviews, and I asked it sixteen years ago. Since then, many of those unrealised projects have seen the light of day – they have been realised. So what, in 2014, are your unrealised projects? Projects that have been too big or too small to be realised, censored projects, self-censored projects, utopic projects that are un-buildable. What are the unbuilt roads of Elmgreen & Dragset?

ID: We did a semi-autobiographical play in New York two years ago that didn't come across in the way we'd intended, and it would be nice to make something that's more autobiographical that would bring a better understanding of who we are. I think the structure of it could follow the structure of our common CV.

ME: I think unrealised projects should have a utopian aura around them. They shouldn't be – or aren't there to be – realised. Maybe they'll be realised post-mortem, but it's good to have things that remain as ideas that you think would be exciting to realise, but you don't *want* to realise because you know the minute you did, you'd be finished.

HUO: Any other projects? Any censorship situations?

ID: No. We're always very persistent. We mostly force people to realise what we want. [Laughs]

ME: I also think that when you've done a lot of exhibitions, people more or less know who you are and I think we've already scared away those who completely disagree with our worldviews, which makes it easier.

ID: Occasionally we have a dream to do something more illustrative, like making a physical version of one of Perec's books that could be entered and touched and would physically surround you. That would be a dream project. Or one of Ibsen's plays – I saw Ibsen's *A Doll's House* in London last year and it was an amazing version. There were many young audience members absolutely gasping for air, seeing this play. And I think, for instance, *The Master Builder* would be interesting to do as some kind of installation.

ME: For the 'Tomorrow' exhibition, it was very important to us to make an exhibition almost like a film-set, like a staging with a script, everything that would be prepared for making a film – but then not making it. And that film would have been a disaster if it were actually made, because it was only intended to be imagined in people's minds. Some things are better just imagined rather than executed.

Performative Constructions

INTERVIEW BY HANS ULRICH OBRIST

HUO: It would be interesting to talk about this collaboration. Douglas Gordon once told me that he thinks the 1990s have seen a promiscuity of collaborations, and your work is perhaps multiple collaborations with other people. How did it happen that you started to put the focus on the collaboration between the two of you, and could you tell me about the beginning of your collaboration?

ID: It started with doing nothing together for a year but being boyfriends. And I was at that time doing theatre performances, and Michael was doing his art on his own. And since we had so many other things in common, and were getting along so well on most matters, we thought that we'd try to combine my theatre experience and Michael's visual-art experience.

HUO: Which year was this?

ID: This was in '95. And I started helping Michael prepare a show in Stockholm. That was because I could knit, and he wanted to do these knitted pieces: some abstract pets, that the art audience could hug and nurse and feel confident with.

ME: But in Stockholm, nobody feels relaxed at openings, so we had to show the audience how to feel confident and how to use these knitted pets, and then everybody thought it was a performance – so it became our first performance, by coincidence.

HUO: What happened next? Was it followed immediately by a second performance? The first time I saw your works, it was in videos of performances you'd done. It was before I saw your exhibitions. Was the collaboration more on a performative level in the beginning?

ME: We were doing many performances in a Nordic context, and we were always curated to be the funny guys in the corner. If some curator wanted to have a more light activity in a very stiff exhibition, he or she called us and asked us to do something.

HUO: So it had to do with a marginalisation within the exhibition context?

ME: Yes, and very much like becoming a stereotype of yourself – being this kind of almost typecast artist: 'Oh, we know what we can expect from these guys.' So it was fun suddenly to make installation works, because that was a big surprise for everybody: 'Oh, they can do art objects!'

ID: You experience different kinds of marginalisation as a gay couple and quite often in the Scandinavian art context, because there are very few gay artists, you feel like you're in a show just as an alibi, or …

ME: Or as an exotic element in something too predictable.

HUO: I once had a discussion about this issue – in terms of the object – with Félix González-Torres, whom I interviewed four or five years ago. He always used this term 'infiltration'. Could you talk about two questions related to this – on the one hand about González-Torres, if he's of importance for you as a sort of reference – and secondly this notion of infiltration in your own activities?

ID: I think Michael should answer, since he met González-Torres.

ME: Yes, in Copenhagen '93.

HUO: Was it when he did that billboard in Denmark?

ME: Yes, I was in this billboard show with him at that time, but I met him just before. He was invited to a really horrible conference or seminar at the Danish Art Academy and was pretty bored. So we hung out and spoke a lot about how gay people suddenly discovered the use of Minimalism as the ultimate kind of infiltration into the history of high art. Minimalism was always the thing that was shown on a large scale in the most important American art institutions after they'd had a tiny little group show of young artists just to give the institution some credibility, to give the impression of not being conservative. Then the museum director could feel safe having this huge Serra exhibition afterwards, that would cost, say, twenty times as much as the young art show. So, dealing with Minimalism was a kind of challenge for a gay person. It was also to break the stereotype image of gay people being interested in camp and being very feminine in their way of expressing themselves.

HUO: So it becomes a critique of this cliché, like Deleuze always said that art is a critique of any cliché?

ME: Indeed. You don't have one homogeneous homosexual culture as a gay person: you're as different from other gay people as anybody else is different from anybody else.

ID: That's also very much the reason why we stopped doing the kind of performances we were doing in the beginning. The performances we did were very important on a personal level and also on the level of artistic development for us, but you felt you were becoming too much of a gay icon, and that's where our *Powerless Structures* series started. That was also an emancipation from this stereotypical image of gay people or being a gay couple.

So we opened up our own artistic expression to include all kinds of material, historical and cultural elements.

ME: It has very much to do with not marginalising oneself. A gay icon is as bad as any icon. It's all about not fulfilling the expectations.

HUO: I once had a discussion with Vito Acconci, about something that's maybe similar to this transition of yours. At a certain stage he decided to appear less himself in the work, so that his presence was more of an absence.

ME: Still, people have the impression or the image of performance – and it's very much in the history of performance itself – that the self or the ego of the performer is very central. It can be the body or it can be the social figure of the performer that's very important, whereas for instance, Acconci and more recent performance artists have taken a step further.

HUO: Whom do you think of among your colleagues?

ME: Actually, no one in the performance field. More artists working in other media. Most of the works that we've done are attempts to make dead materials come alive, like painting a gallery white for twelve hours, or making this temporary white cube by painting the walls of a transparent glass box from the inside, the piece that we did at the Secession in Vienna where we created a white cube that lasted for only maybe fifteen minutes. In live acts like these, our personal presence is only to keep the material moving.

We're only taking part in the process of the performance, along with the materials and the objects. So we don't expose ourselves as absolute focal points in our live acts. Our egos and our bodies are no more relevant for the reading of our performances than they are for the reading of our objects and installation works. In the performances we're taking part in a process that's going on with the material.

HUO: But did you ever think about, in terms of the different notion of time, the viewer basically also playing a bigger part?

ID: Our works are very simple; they are, in a way, minimal, and this is not to make a reduction, but to open up – not so much to open us up towards the audience, but to keep it open for the audience to read things that they'd like to read into this open field.

ME: And in that way, we're very traditional, because we're not calculating the reactions of the audience. We're not making entirely interactive works that demand a certain behaviour of the audience, like 'push this button', or 'step here' kind of things. We're creating the artwork, and then we're not sure about what the reaction of the audience will be. We're not figuring anything out beforehand.

ID: In Paris we made this completely white carpet, and you had to pass over it to see the rest of the exhibition. You'd expect that some people would be reluctant to step on the carpet, but we couldn't be sure. I think the reactions were different from person to person.

You felt like, 'Should I step on this or not?' After all, you'd put your dirty footprints on it. And maybe it's also a generational thing, people's reactions: some people are used to going to so-called young, contemporary art shows – they're used to interactive works – and wouldn't mind stepping on it, but maybe other people would be reluctant to do it. Maybe they have too much respect for the artwork.

HUO: It was the before and after that was amazing about your 'Nuit Blanche' piece. When we installed your piece, we all took off our shoes in order not to make your white carpet dirty, and the very moment the exhibition opened, and the carpet was still in a virgin state, the audience hardly dared to pass by your piece and to step on the carpet. And then thousands and thousands of people walked on it and left their traces, and it was suddenly completely covered with footprints.

ME: That's exactly what I call the traditional element: that you're not able to predict what will happen with the work, that you have this kind of old-fashioned excitement. I really like that.

HUO: Robert Musil once said, that art often occurs where you expect it least.

ME: And as an artist you must be ready to receive a lot of different reactions to the work, accepting the chaotic conditions of perception.

HUO: Also unusual events?

ME: Yes. When we did our performance in Paris, there was this child who was going on and on interfering with our performance, playing with the yarn, and so on. But being very sure of what we were doing, we were just like, 'This is OK.' People could separate what we were doing from the interruption of this child suddenly participating in the performance – and in this way the spectators had two different experiences at the same time. As a performer, it doesn't help if you're totally freaking out if something unexpected is going on.

HUO: Do you have other examples of unusual events, of things that you wouldn't have expected?

ID: When we did our *Twelve Hours of White Paint* performance in Mexico, the paint quality was so bad: it wasn't exactly white, it was more kind of grey, and it was very watery and very chalky. But the atmosphere was so good, and suddenly it became something else, because we were these two white guys trashing a white cube gallery with white paint in Mexico. So it had a lot of other connotations.

HUO: Could you tell me about your *Powerless Structures*? You wrote a text about it, but not about how you arrived at the title. I'd be very interested to know how you defined this series, and if you knew from the beginning exactly where it would lead?

ME: In Foucault's *History of Sexuality*, he writes that no structure is able to suppress anybody – not the structure itself. It's only how you deal with the structures already there, and all structures can be altered or mutated.

That was very much an inspiration for us – to discover that everything is just structures that could be something else – the patterns could be different. It was just a question of imagination. And when it's just a question of imagination, the visual-art field is such a good area in which to work with these things in a very concrete and very simple way. So we started making these suggestions, that everything – from social and political structures to architectural and cultural structures – could be something more exciting and more open, and to make these suggestions we just needed small elements to start the change.

HUO: So basically to change the rules of the game?

ME: The game is a dynamic game. It's possible to combine the structures in billions of different ways in every field.

HUO: In architecture, for example?

ID: The architectural frame of a gallery or a gay bar, for instance. It could basically be anything – the social structures or whatever. And that's also how we've come to make pieces that involve both the art-institutional structures and some basic gay social structures, and tested what happens if you combine these. The piece that you've seen at Kunstraum der Universität Lüneburg deals with this. Here, we made two sex cabins that you normally find in the back room of gay bars or in porn kinos and we placed them in the white cube context. When you enter the cabins you can see the rest of the exhibition through the peep holes – to see and to be seen.

HUO: Active and passive viewing.

ME: And it's very much about the voyeuristic situation. A trained art audience may feel on safe ground going into a gallery space, but they'll be totally alienated when going into the back room of a gay bar, whereas a lot of the gay crowd who are, uh, consulting the back rooms will be totally alienated going into a gallery space. Combining these two kinds of architecture seemed interesting to us, because it points out that you don't have spaces such as queer spaces, and you don't have spaces such as art spaces. You only have spaces that are occupied for a certain period by artistic behaviour, and you have places that are occupied by queer activity for a certain time. The borderlines aren't that strict. They're much more fragile than we imagine them.

HUO: Acconci, in an interview I made with him, said that the biggest mistake is that people always think that spaces are God-given – they think it's a public space while it's really about what you make: you make it public.

ID: If we could just come to a point where people were more anarchistic in that way, so that they no longer believed in structures being able to suppress them or in spaces being predestined for a specific purpose, then I think we'd have come a long way.

HUO: So could one say that the object isn't an absolute reality, or not a self-fulfillment, but is more like a trigger for dialogues.

ME: I don't think anything can be seen as an absolute reality, neither an art object nor anything else. The dialogue is of great importance. But I don't agree with 'the object just being a trigger', actually. I'm very fond of the presence of the object, and I'm very fond of it even in a performance context. It has itself this kind of very close communication with the audience. I don't feel that the spoken word or mental communication is any better than presenting an object. I don't have a problem with materials, so I don't like this distinction between hardware and software. What's most important: an apple or a spoken word? Well, if you're hungry ...

HUO: What I think is very interesting about your work over the last couple of years, is that your installation works also have this performative side, this combination of object and action, like in Kathrin Rhomberg's 'Junge Szene' at the Secession in Vienna, with the glass box painted white, or even in your Berlin piece in the Biennial, the wishing well. Tomorrow there will be this small performance of you throwing coins into the well. Then the action will be frozen as an image, and for the rest of the exhibition period one can see the installation with the coins, the materiality. Your work brings together different possibilities: there's the potential action to happen, there's the event, the live event, and there's the trace of the event in its materiality.

ME: Almost any cultural object is performative. If you take a coffee pot, it's waiting for us to make coffee in it. If you have a chair, it's waiting for you to sit on it.

And all the nature that surrounds you is cultivated now, especially with the new gene technology. In a couple of years, you won't be able to eat a carrot that hasn't been genetically manipulated – it can't grow without that – so it's also performative in a way. So, I don't see the objects that we're doing as totally apart from the performances we're doing. It's all part of the same system.

ID: It might be that people who also know our performances read more performative things into the installation pieces.

ME: I think we share with a lot of the artists of today – and in fact all the way back to Duchamp painting a mustache on the *Mona Lisa* – this attitude that art is far from the static masterpiece, but instead communication that can change all the time. Duchamp saw that painting as something that was screaming to be changed, so he added his own statement to the work and it became a sort of interactive act. A lot of times, when I'm looking at paintings I feel like making a little green figure or something in the corner of the canvas, to keep it alive by changing it.

HUO: To add or to subtract?

ME: It depends.

HUO: Let's talk more about the Berlin piece, about this 'Fontana Tremens' that leads us to the Fontana di Trevi – Baroque meets Minimalism.

ID: It's a pond, a wishing well, right outside the entrance of the exhibition space, in front of the stairs, and you can step on it on your way up because it's covered with a thick safety-glass plate. There are coins at the bottom of it, and there's this very thick glass plate on top, so you can't throw any more coins in there – that means there are no more wishes to be made. Tomorrow it will be possible for people who happen to be there at twelve o'clock for the installation to make their wishes for Berlin. After that, the work is sealed. But then it's possible to walk on it, over its blue water.

ME: It's kind of in-between a romantic wishing well and a swimming pool, because it's square, and it has this bluish water inside, and underwater lighting. We got the coins from the Danish National Bank, and they're coins that haven't yet been stamped with the image of the queen and their value. So actually, they're value-less coins. You don't throw a specific amount of money into the pool. But it's fun that you call it Baroque, because I think it fits with the location, which is this totally over-the-top historic building with a lot of different styles. It's funny that these contradictions melt together to create a new kind of harmony when you don't respect the borderlines of logic.

HUO: I was wondering if you could tell me about your favourite unrealised projects – projects that haven't been realised for certain reasons: because maybe the funding wasn't there, or maybe they've been censored, or maybe they've been forgotten. Or if you have projects which are more utopian, too big to happen?

ME: We have one piece with turning walls and static/ permanent walls, an architectural piece that's meant to divide up an exhibition space, where the turning walls will create an ever-changing architecture, or structure for the rooms. It will divide the rooms up in different ways all the time. And this is totally impossible to produce anywhere. It would go into the physical structure of the museum, which would damage it, and it would cost a fortune to produce. But it's such a great project to work on, just for fun, developing it, making it more ridiculous than it was before, more utopian, and it's kind of an ongoing project.

This is a slightly edited version of the interview originally published in *Powerless Structures – works by Michael Elmgreen and Ingar Dragset*, Nifca, Helsinki, 1998, pp.27-43.

ANDREW BERARDINI

born 1982 in California, is a writer and occasional curator born in the US. He writes about the permeability between imagination and reality, in mostly fictive essays, as well as the art of Los Angeles where he lives. Previously a curator at LAXART and the Armory Center and an editor at *Semiotext(e)*, he is currently LA Editor of *Mousse*, Senior Editor of *Artslant*, teacher at the Mountain School of Arts, and founder of the *Art Book Review*. Publications to which he has contributed include *Artforum*, *LA Weekly*, *Public Fiction* and *Purple*, as well as numerous catalogues. Recently, he has organised exhibitions at Palais de Tokyo, Castello di Rivoli, MOCA Los Angeles, and the Church of the Holy Shroud in Turin. A finalist for the Premio Bonaldi and winner of an Andy Warhol / Creative Capital Grant for Art Writers in 2013, he is currently at work on a book about colour.

IWONA BLAZWICK

born 1955 in London, has been Director of the Whitechapel Gallery, London, since 2001 and is a curator, critic and lecturer. She was formerly curator at Tate Modern and Head of Exhibitions at London's ICA, as well as working as an independent curator in Europe and Japan. Blazwick was also a Commissioning Editor for Phaidon Press and is series editor of Whitechapel Gallery/MIT Documents of Contemporary Art.

She has published extensively on individual artists, themes and movements in modern and contemporary art, exhibition histories and art institutions.

SUSANNE CHRISTENSEN

born 1969 in Copenhagen, Denmark, studied creative writing at Skrivekunstakademiet in Bergen, Norway, and has a Master's degree in comparative literature from the University of Bergen. In the early 2000s she was a co-editor of the Norwegian small press Gasspedal, and now works as a critic for the daily newspaper *Klassekampen* and at Kunstkritikk.no. She is also a columnist for the literature magazine *Vagant*. In 2011 she was awarded Critic of the Year by The Norwegian Critics' Association, the same year in which her collection of essays and reviews *Den ulne avantgarde. Kritiske tekster fra 00-tallet* was published by Flamme Forlag, Oslo. Currently she is working on a collection of travel essays from Russia and America with a focus on feminist grassroots activism. She lives in Berlin.

RUTH DIREKTOR

born 1956 in Tel Aviv, studied art history and classical studies at Tel Aviv University. From 1984 to 2008 she was an art critic, writing regularly for several of the most prominent newspapers and weekly magazines in Israel. Her book *Contemporary Art I Am Talking to You* was published in 2005.

Her articles and reviews about contemporary art, both Israeli and international, have been published in many catalogues and other publications. Throughout the years, she has taught courses at different art academies focusing on issues of contemporary art. Since the early 1990s she has worked as an independent curator, and since 2005 has been the curator of The Art Gallery of the University of Haifa, the curator of The Gallery of Bezalel Academy of Art and Design in Tel Aviv, and then the Chief Curator of Haifa Museum of Art. She is currently the Curator of Contemporary Art at Tel Aviv Museum of Art.

BRUCE WILLIS FERGUSON

born in Alberta, Canada received his BA in Art History from the University of Saskatchewan and his MA in Communications from McGill University in Montreal. He is vice chairman of LB Media in New York, a print and online publishing company. He has been the Dean of the School of Humanities and Social Sciences at the American University in Cairo, Egypt, and served as the Dean of the School of Arts at Columbia University, as well as president and executive director of the New York Academy of Art. Ferguson has curated exhibitions for institutions such as the Louisiana Museum of Modern Art, Copenhagen; Barbican Centre, London; Vancouver Art Gallery; and the Institute of Contemporary Art, Boston. He has also organised exhibitions for the international biennials of São Paulo, Sydney, Venice and Istanbul. He has served as curatorial consultant for the Vancouver Cultural Olympiad (2010); Albright Knox Art Gallery, Buffalo; and Art Gallery of Ontario, Toronto. Ferguson has written for *Canadian Art*, *Artforum*, *Art in America*, *Flash Art*, *Bomb Magazine*, *Art Press*, *Border Crossings* and *Parachute*, and is co-editor of the seminal textbook anthology *Thinking About Exhibitions* (1996). He has an honorary doctorate from the Kansas City Art Institute.

MASSIMILIANO GIONI

born 1973 in Busto Arsizio, Italy, is the Artistic Director of the Nicola Trussardi Foundation in Milan and the Associate Director of the New Museum in New York. He has curated numerous international exhibitions, including the 55th Venice Biennale (2013), the 8th Gwangju Biennale (2010), the 4th Berlin Biennale (2006) and Manifesta 5 (2004).

MARTIN HERBERT

born 1973 in Wakefield, UK, is a writer and critic based in Tunbridge Wells and Berlin. He writes regularly for *Artforum*, *frieze* and *Art Monthly*, and is an associate editor of *Art Review*. His writing has also appeared in catalogues for the Museum of Modern Art, New York, the Hayward Gallery and Tate Britain, London, among others. His monograph on Mark Wallinger was published by Thames & Hudson in 2011; *The Uncertainty Principle*, a book of essays, is forthcoming from Sternberg Press.

SHANNON JACKSON

born 1967, is the Director of the Arts Research Center (ARC) at UC-Berkeley, where she is also the Goldman Professor of Rhetoric and of Theater, Dance, and Performance Studies. Her research focuses primarily on inter-art collaboration and on art and sociality, including publications such as *Lines of Activity* (2000), *Professing Performance* (2004), and *Social Works: Performing Art, Supporting Publics* (2011). Jackson is currently finishing a book on intermedia performance for MIT Press and has started a new book, *The Way We Perform Now*, supported by a 2014/2015 John Simon Guggenheim Fellowship. As ARC Director, she has organised numerous symposia, publications and artist residencies, and serves as a board member of Cal Performances, the Berkeley Art Museum, The English Institute, and the UC Institute for Research in the Arts.

GUNNAR B. KVARAN

born 1955 in Reykjavík, Iceland, studied art history at l'Université de Provence, Aix-en-Provence, France, where he received his PhD in 1986. He has been Director of Astrup Fearnley Museum since 2001, prior to which he was the Director of The Ásmundur Sveinsson Sculpture Museum in Reykjavík (1983–89), The Reykjavík Art Museum (1989–97) and Bergen Art Museum (1997–2001). From 1981 to 1985 he was an art critic for *Dagblaðið Vísir* in Reykjavík. He was the curator of the Icelandic Pavilion at the Venice Biennale in 1984, 1986, 1988 and 1990, co-curator of The 2nd Moscow Biennale of Contemporary Art in 2007 (in collaboration with Hans Ulrich Obrist and Daniel Birnbaum) and curator of the 12th Lyon Biennale in 2013. He recently curated the following exhibitions: *Imagine Brazil* (together with Hans Ulrich Obrist and Thierry Raspail, 2013), *Elmgreen & Dragset: Biography* (together with Kjersti Solbakken, 2014) and *L'Europe des Artistes* (together with Hans Ulrich Obrist and Thomas Boutoux, 2014).

QUINN LATIMER

born 1978 in Venice, California, studied sculpture, art history and poetry at Sarah Lawrence College and Columbia University's School of the Arts, New York. She currently works as a poet, critic, editor and occasional curator in Basel, Switzerland. She is the author of the poetry collection *Rumored Animals* (2012), and *Sarah Lucas: Describe This Distance* (2013), and is a regular contributor to *Artforum* and a contributing editor to *Frieze*. She is the editor of *Paul Sietsema: Interviews on Films and Works* (2012), and co-editor of *Stories, Myths, Ironies, and Other Songs: Conceived, Directed, Edited, and Produced by M. Auder* (2014); *Olinka, or Where Movement Is Created* (2013); and *No Core: Pamela Rosenkranz* (2012). Her readings and lectures have been held widely, including at Astrup Fearnley Museet, Oslo; Chisenhale Gallery, London; Whitechapel

Gallery, London; dOCUMENTA (13), Kassel; Witte de With Center for Contemporary Art, Rotterdam; and Kunsthalle Zurich. Her videos and text works have also recently been featured in exhibitions at the Venice Architecture Biennale; CRAC Alsace; Fondation d'Enterprise Galeries Lafayette, Paris; and CCA Ujazdowski Castle, Warsaw. Latimer teaches at Geneva's Haute école d'art et de design (HEAD).

HANS ULRICH OBRIST

born 1968 in Zurich, Switzerland, is co-director of the Serpentine Galleries, London. Prior to this, he was the Curator of the Musée d'art moderne de la ville de Paris. Since his first show *World Soup* (The Kitchen Show) in 1991, he has curated more than 250 exhibitions. In 2009 Obrist was made Honorary Fellow of the Royal Institute of British Architects (RIBA), and in 2011 received the CCS Bard Award for Curatorial Excellence. He has lectured internationally at academic and art institutions, and is contributing editor to several magazines and journals. His recent publications include *A Brief History of Curating, Everything You Always Wanted to Know About Curating But Were Afraid to Ask*; *Do It: The Compendium*; *Think Like Clouds*; *Ai Weiwei Speaks* and *Ways of Curating*, along with new volumes of his *Conversation Series*.

MARIANNE TORP

born 1964 in Copenhagen, Denmark, studied art history at the University of Copenhagen and Columbia University in New York. She is Chief Curator and Senior Researcher at the SMK, the National Gallery of Denmark, where has been running the project space x-rummet since 2001, commissioning numerous new works and artist's projects as well as large-scale exhibitions. One of the very first exhibitions at x-rummet was a project by Elmgreen & Dragset.

Imprint

This reader is published in conjunction with the three-part exhibition:

Elmgreen & Dragset
Biography

Astrup Fearnley Museet, Oslo
21 March, 2014 – 24 August, 2014

SMK – National Gallery of
Denmark, Copenhagen
19 September, 2014 – 4 January, 2015

Tel Aviv Museum of Art, Tel Aviv
12 March, 2015 – 29 August, 2015

This book is a collaboration between

Astrup Fearnley Museet, SMK –
National Gallery of Denmark
and Tel Aviv Museum of Art

Curators Astrup Fearnley Museet:
Gunnar B. Kvaran, Kjersti Solbakken

Curator SMK – National Gallery
of Denmark: Marianne Torp

Curators Tel Aviv Museum of Art:
Suzanne Landau, Ruth Direktor

Catalogue

Editors: Gunnar B. Kvaran,
Kjersti Solbakken

Managing editors: Kjersti Solbakken,
Hanne Beate Ueland

Copy editor and proofreader:
Melissa Larner

Translators: Daria Kassovsky (Direktor),
René Lauritsen (Christensen, Torp)

Coordinator: Anita Iannacchione

Photo credits: Carla Åhlander (121); Bórkur Arnarson (125 bottom); Anders Sune Berg (98–101, 106, 108–109, 113 bottom, 115–119, 128, 133); Danny Bright (141 bottom); Thor Brødreskift (126–127); Neil Thomas Douglas (135); Elmgreen & Dragset (136 bottom, 142 bottom); Leonie Felle (137 bottom); Murat Germen (143); Juan Carlos Guerra / Roberto Caldeyro Stajano (124 bottom); Wolfgang Günzel (124 top); James O Jenkins (132 – Elmgreen & Dragset, *Powerless Structures, Fig. 101,* Commissioned for the Mayor of London's Fourth Plinth Programme); Matthias Kolb, Berlin (140); Kunstnernes Hus, Oslo (120); Nic Lehoux (114); Jannes Linders (137 top); Armin Linke (105 bottom); Roman März (97); Cameron McNee (110–111); Udo Meinel (104); ONUK (102–103, 105 top); Mariano Peuser (130); Bent Ryberg (142 top); Oren Slor (131); Sandra Stemmer (107); Studio Blu, Milano (122–123); Andreas Szlavik (125 top); Tot en met ontwerpen (138–139); Elmar Vestner (134, 136 top); Stephen White (129); Alessandro Zambianchi (112); Guillaume Ziccarelli (113 top); Jens Ziehe (141 top)

Design: Archive Appendix, Chiara Figone

Print: Hinkelstein druck, Berlin

ISBN 978-3-943620-18-4

Astrup Fearnley Museet

Astrup Fearnley Museet
Strandpromenaden 2, 0252 Oslo,
POB 2074 Vika, NO-0125 Oslo, Norway
Phone: +47 2293 6061
www.afmuseet.no

The museum is generously supported by
the Foundation Thomas Fearnley, Heddy
and Nils Astrup, and Astrup Fearnley A/S

© 2014 Elmgreen & Dragset, Berlin;
Archive Books, Berlin; and the authors
© 2014 Astrup Fearnley Museet, Oslo;
SMK – National Gallery of Denmark,
Copenhagen; Tel Aviv Museum of Art,
Tel Aviv
© 2014 for the reproduced works by
Elmgreen & Dragset: VG Bild-Kunst,
Bonn / Copy-Dan Billedkunst, Copenhagen
as well as the photographers and their heirs

Published by
Archive Books
Dieffenbachstraße 31
10967 Berlin
mail@archivebooks.org
www.archivebooks.org

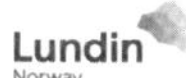 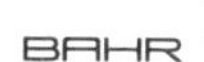 

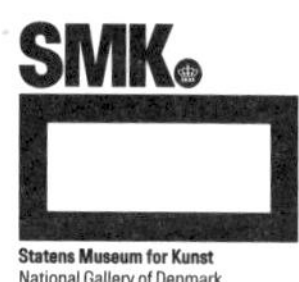

SMK – National Gallery of Denmark
Sølvgade 48-50,
1307 Copenhagen K, Denmark
Phone: +45 3374 8494
www.smk.dk

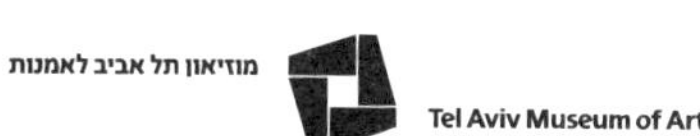

Tel Aviv Museum of Art
27 Shaul Hamelech Blvd, POB 33288
61332012 Tel Aviv, Israel
Phone: +972 (0)3 6077020
www.tamuseum.org.il